THE
BUILD-TO-RENT
STRATEGY

A Guide to a Successful Rental Property Construction

NATALIE CLOUTIER

For more information, email info@thenewbuildcouple.com.

ISBN: 979-8-89694-510-9 - Ebook
ISBN: 979-8-89694-511-6 - Paperback

CONTENTS

DEDICATION

I want to express my deepest gratitude to my husband, Rob. Without him, this book—and everything we've built together—would not exist. His unwavering support, dedication, and partnership have been the backbone of our journey. Every success we celebrate is a reflection of the sacrifices we've made and the vision we've shared. Thank you for being my rock, my greatest ally, and my constant source of strength. This book is as much yours as it is mine.

To my mom—my greatest cheerleader and behind-the-scenes advisor. Her wisdom, encouragement, and listening ear have been invaluable throughout this journey. She has always believed in me, even when I doubted myself, and her guidance has made all the difference.

And to everyone who has supported me along the way—you know who you are—thank you for your encouragement, inspiration, and belief throughout this crazy journey.

DISCLOSURE

The information and materials provided in this book are for informational and reference purposes only. They are based on our personal experiences and insights into our local market. While we strive for accuracy and clarity, as well as a general guidance to reflect broader markets, the contents of this book should not be considered professional advice.

Readers are strongly encouraged to consult with qualified professionals, including but not limited to attorneys, accountants, financial advisors, and other relevant experts, before making any decisions or entering into any agreements or investments. Every market and situation is unique, and professional guidance can help ensure your choices are well-informed and tailored to your circumstances.

We disclaim any liability for actions taken based on the information contained within this book. Investing and construction involve risks, and the reader assumes full responsibility for any decisions made.

INTRODUCTION

For many, financial security feels like a distant dream. The traditional path—working a stable job, saving diligently, and maybe investing in the stock market—seems like the only option. Yet, with the rising cost of living, stagnant wages, and increasing debt, that route no longer guarantees true freedom. And with everything happening in the world—from mass job losses during the pandemic to rising tariffs threatening industries—there has never been a better time to take control of your financial future. Relying on governments and employers is no longer a safe bet, and most likely never was. The only real security comes from building something for yourself.

Most known real estate investing strategies revolve around buying outdated properties, renovating them, and either renting or flipping them for a profit. But what if there was a different approach—one that doesn't rely on hunting for underpriced deals in an increasingly competitive market? What if you could create your own opportunities instead of waiting for the perfect property to appear? There's a proven strategy that not only builds wealth but also creates true financial independence—one that generates income regardless of market fluctuations or job security. That's exactly what this book is about: A roadmap to leveraging the power of Build-to-Rent (BTR) real estate investments. And we did it all, starting from a humble beginning with zero dollars.

Fresh out of college, my husband Rob and I were 20 years old, earning entry-level salaries of just $30,000 each. We knew we wanted more, but we had no idea how to achieve it. We weren't born into wealth. We didn't have financial backers or trust funds. What we did have was a willingness to learn, work hard, and take risks.

Looking back on our journey, I can't help but feel an overwhelming sense of pride for what my husband and I have accomplished. Not only did we juggle full-time jobs, but we also devoted any free time we had to building homes from the ground up, and it was far from easy. It demanded a great deal of effort, we overcame numerous obstacles and made sacrifices to get to where we are today. We put everything we had into our investment business, and I'm impressed with what we've achieved together. And, we're not finished yet. We continuously strive toward new objectives and every other day we generate fresh ideas to improve and grow our business, as well as ourselves.

We do this not because we lack the money and feel the need to continue, but because we developed a true passion for this business. We are still active investors, but we finally have that freedom of flexible time and choosing what our schedules look like each week. Like choosing to book last minute trips every couple of months or escaping to the cottage in the middle of the workweek. Heck, parts of this book were written from a balcony in Florida overlooking a beautiful pool and sunset, on a cruise ship in the Mediterranean, and from our cottage by the lake— while three of our build projects were being completed by our team. So yes, life is good today. But it's been quite a journey to get here.

It started when Rob and I met in college while studying architectural technology. However our real estate journey began in 2013, just a couple months after graduating, when we purchased our first home—a basement-level condo. We got accepted for the mortgage through a government program for first-time homebuyers that needed no down payment. At the time, we were thrilled just to get approved for a mortgage and we didn't realize that we were trading a 0$ down payment for a higher interest rate. Add on the condo fees that were already announced to increase as soon as we moved in, and we realized maybe it was a poor financial decision. Our budget felt too tight. Within months, we wanted out.

My parents then revealed how they built their first homes using "auto construction" loans. These loans allowed them to replace a down payment with sweat equity—contributing physical labor and management to reduce costs. They also explained how designing a home that had a basement apartment with rental income, was the only way they stayed afloat during hard times. This revelation was a turning point.

Little did we all know that that recipe would shape our entire future success. Next thing we knew, we were meeting with a financial advisor and securing such a loan to build our home. The catch? We had to do a lot of the work ourselves.

However, selling our condo wasn't easy in our sluggish market. Instead of walking away at a loss, we found tenants willing to rent it for $1,200 per month—even though it meant taking on negative cash flow of $300/month. It was terrifying. We had no experience being landlords, and we certainly didn't feel like real estate investors. I'll dive more into this later, for now let's fast forward.

After we managed to build our home, we added a two bedroom basement apartment to help pay expenses, making us landlords for the second time. Now that we had done a new construction and had renters in both places, we started to notice the benefits of rental income. Both tenants paid for almost our entire mortgage expenses. Yes we had a 300$ loss on the condo, but seeing as we had almost nothing left to pay for living in our home, we could easily cover that cost now. On top of that, we had two properties instead of one now, while living in a newly built dream home. We quickly recognized the potential to create a business around all of this, prompting us to continue building more homes. Eventually, we weren't just landlords anymore—we were real estate developers.

We also learned early on one of the most important lessons in finance: The difference between good debt and bad debt. Good debt—like a mortgage on a rental property—can generate income or appreciate in value, providing returns greater than the cost of borrowing. On the other hand, bad debt—like credit cards or car loans or condo fees—drains your resources without offering a financial return. Avoiding bad debt early on helped us stay focused and build a solid foundation for our business.

Fast forward to today, and we've built a portfolio of rental properties that gave us financial independence before turning 30 years old. But more importantly, we've built a lifestyle where our money works for us—where we have the time and freedom to live on our own terms. Of course, it was not easy. Our sacrifices early on to avoid bad debt were significant and included working long hours, cutting back on social activities, driving used cars to avoid payments, and having a small wedding. But looking back, we would do it all over again. Today, we see it clearly.

While our journey may not have been very conventional compared to how most people spend their twenties, we were able to learn a ton early in life. Building and holding can genuinely be a rewarding venture. If done right, over time investing and building property can provide a steady stream of passive income and long-term wealth, not to mention a sense of pride in creating something from nothing.

WHY THIS BOOK?

This book is the guide we wish we had when we started. It's not about flipping houses or gambling on market appreciation. It's about a proven, repeatable strategy to build long-term wealth through Build-to-Rent (BTR) real estate.

Inside, you'll learn:

✓ How to find and evaluate land deals

✓ How to design and build rentals for maximum profitability

✓ The numbers that actually matter (and how to avoid costly mistakes)

✓ How to finance, budget, and manage a construction project—even with no experience

If you've ever thought, "I'd love to invest in real estate through new construction, but I don't know where to start"—this book is for you.

I won't lie—this path isn't easy. It requires work, patience, and strategic decision-making. But what's the alternative? Working 40+ years in a job you don't love, doing 40+ hours a week, juggling the never ending monthly expenses while also hoping you're saving enough for retirement?

Real estate is one of the most powerful wealth-building tools available—but only if you take action.

So the question is: Are you ready to build your future?

CHAPTER 1

WHAT IS THE BUILD-TO-RENT (BTR) STRATEGY?

It's funny because what I'm doing today—designing, building, and monitoring construction sites—was exactly what I imagined myself doing when I was younger. I had a passion for design and construction, but I always pictured myself doing this work for others, being hired by wealthier individuals. Back then, I thought building new properties was a big, complicated, risky, and out-of-reach concept. I never imagined I'd own over $13 million in real estate (and growing), developing and finding creative financing solutions for multi-million-dollar projects, while collaborating with city officials and sometimes even politicians. Through my younger eyes, anyone who did that seemed like a phony—a poser pretending to be wealthy, when really the mafia was after them for high debt.

I actually come from a long line of builders, yet everything I know about financial stability and real estate investing today, I've learned through my own experiences—aside from the initial advice and guidance my parents provided in the beginning about building using your labor and having a basement apartment for additional income.

My grandfather was a builder, who developed dozens of homes and subdivisions with partners, but he declared bankruptcy in the 80s. My uncle also dabbled in development, though I'm not too clear on his history. My parents built four homes in four years before having my sister and me. The first three homes were built to sell until they settled on the fourth where they lived for over 30 years. They decided to retire from building houses when my older sister was born.

Then, my mom opened up a home daycare which she ran for 20 years. My dad worked as an Estimator for a disaster restoration company, until eventually he started his small restoration and renovation business. By the time I came into the world, four years after my sister, no one in my family was building or developing anymore.

My parents had built a basement apartment in that fourth home to support my grandparents through their bankruptcy. My grandparents lived in that apartment until the end of their lives. At the time, I didn't understand the full story. When you're born into something, it all seems very normal—until one day you realize maybe it's not. To me, they were just my grandparents living in the same house as us which I thought was really fun. It wasn't until I was well into my own building journey that I learned about my grandfather's bankruptcy.

He had once been successful, but poor cash flow management and the unexpected market shift of the 1980s wiped him out. You see, back in my grandfather's day, financing was less about navigating the strict policies and bureaucracies we deal with today. Instead, it was more about who could entertain and impress the bankers at soirées, and my grandfather definitely knew how to throw parties and how to entertain guests. This casual relationship with financing, combined with the oil crisis and loose monetary policies of the 1970s, led to an inflation surge. Similar to what we experienced with the 2020 pandemic, the 1980s saw aggressive interest rate hikes to combat inflation. Isn't it interesting to see how truly cyclical the real estate market is?

After learning about this, I looked at other builders from that era, and I realized they shared a common factor: They weren't holding on to their real estate. They were focused on building to sell for quicker profits.

My family's history made me cautious, as I had learnt a powerful lesson: You can't build wealth by just building to sell—you have to hold onto properties and let them appreciate over time. While building to sell might yield quicker returns, it often comes with high transactional costs and constant market risks. Builders who prioritize short-term gains without a long-term strategy frequently encounter cash flow issues, especially during unexpected market shifts. Although this approach can bring substantial profits quickly, inadequate financial planning—like failing to save for downturns or manage debt—can lead to devastating losses in tough economic times.

Unlike traditional fix-and-flip or build-to-sell methods that prioritize short-term gains, the BTR, or sometimes I like to call it the Build & Hold Strategy, involves constructing properties from the ground up, retaining ownership, and leasing them for steady, passive income. It's a visionary strategy that begins with acquiring vacant land, providing investors with a blank canvas to create income-generating assets. I'm grateful that Rob and I adopted this strategy. The hold part especially has since become our guiding principle in real estate. This powerful, time-tested approach emphasizes long-term ownership and rental income, creating lasting wealth and financial freedom.

That said, I'm not suggesting that the BTR (or Build & Hold) strategy is risk-free and I'm not saying you should never sell. We've sold several properties we built during our journey because it just made sense to exchange low cash flow properties to recycle capital and reinvest in a better ROI. Sometimes it's essential to clean up the portfolio, but we only sell when necessary. And like any investment, holding still comes with its own set of challenges, including market fluctuations, mismanagement of the construction process, lack of due diligence, and financing problems. However, when done right, it paints a picture of more sustainable growth and long-term stability.

BUILD OR RENOVATE? WHY NEW CONSTRUCTION WINS EVERY TIME FOR US

Many real estate investors are drawn to purchasing existing properties to improve and add value. But while the potential rewards are tempting, we believe new builds have a distinct advantage in maximizing net worth and cash flow. Let's dive into why we favor new construction and how it stacks up against renovations.

THE VALUE GAME: CREATE YOUR OWN DEALS

New builds allow you to create your own deals. For us, it's been like finding a loophole for generating value on our terms. The biggest challenge with renovations is finding properties that still have enough equity left to justify the investment, especially in competitive markets. Add in the fact that rental laws can make it difficult to vacate tenants in places like Ontario, where you can't simply evict someone to renovate and raise rents, and suddenly the idea of buying an older property seems less appealing.

With new construction, you start with a clean slate. You can design the property to meet market demands from day one, without worrying about inherited tenants, old layouts, or dealing with costly, hidden repairs.

QUALITY OVER QUANTITY: A HIGHER RETURN PER UNIT

Let's look at the numbers. We've found that new builds often result in a higher return per unit. For example, I know someone who owned an 88-unit portfolio worth $15 million, averaging $170,000 per unit. Their properties were older and located in a market with similar property values. In comparison, our $12 million portfolio had just 38 units, averaging a value of around $315,000 per unit. By focusing on fewer, high-value new builds, we reduce operational costs and simplify management. This not only lowers expenses but also improves cash flow, as these properties attract higher-quality tenants and command stronger rental income. As a result, we've been able to scale back on property management while boosting the overall profitability of each unit.

CUSTOMIZATION AND CONTROL: YOUR VISION, YOUR TERMS

One of the most exciting aspects of building new is the ability to customize everything. From the layout to fire separation to installing separate meters for each unit, you get full control over design and construction. This is where we get to create a property that aligns perfectly with our goals. We can design for functionality, maximizing privacy, and incorporating all the latest amenities to meet market demand.

By contrast, with renovations, you're constrained by the existing layout, structural challenges, and outdated systems. Building from scratch eliminates those limitations and allows you to design exactly what the market is asking for—whether that's energy-efficient features, open-concept layouts, or larger units to attract long-term tenants.

NO INHERITED TENANTS: A CLEAN SLATE

Another huge advantage of new builds is that there are no inherited tenants. Buying a property with tenants in place creates potential issues—unhappy tenants, rent increases, evictions, and a whole host of headaches that come with managing a tenant base that didn't sign on with you in mind. Even with a property manager, you can't fully avoid these issues, especially in markets with strict rental laws.

By building from scratch, you're starting fresh with a tenant base that's excited to move into a brand-new space. This allows you to create a better rental experience for both you and your tenants.

MODERNIZATION: ATTRACTING LONG-TERM TENANTS

New homes are more attractive to tenants seeking long-term housing solutions. With modern layouts, updated energy-efficient appliances, and new building materials, your property will stand out in the rental market. Not only does this increase your chances of securing high-quality tenants, but it also gives you an edge in terms of rent prices. A well-designed, brand-new property will be able to command higher rents and draw in a stable, long-term tenant base.

LOWER MAINTENANCE, FEWER SURPRISES: THE LONG-TERM ADVANTAGE

One of the most compelling reasons to build new is the lower maintenance and fewer surprises that come with it. Older properties often come with unexpected repairs and breakdowns, from plumbing issues to aging roofs and electrical systems. With new construction, you know exactly what's behind the walls and systems from day one. While there may be some initial adjustments in the first year, you can rest assured that the property is in top shape and will require far fewer repairs compared to older homes.

This translates into less stress, fewer unexpected expenses, and ultimately, more cash flow in your pocket.

BUILDING FOR THE FUTURE: LONG-TERM GROWTH AND STABILITY

The demand for rental housing continues to rise, fueled by demographic shifts and the growing challenge of homeownership affordability. Purpose-built rentals, especially new construction, are perfectly positioned to meet this demand. By carefully selecting locations and designing your properties to align with market needs, you can watch your asset value grow and enjoy long-term equity appreciation.

The BTR strategy isn't just about building homes—it's about building wealth. With new construction, you're investing in a property that is likely to increase in value over time, giving you a solid foundation for future growth. And with the potential for tax benefits in certain jurisdictions, new builds become an even more attractive option for investors looking to scale their portfolios.

DIVERSIFICATION AND RISK MITIGATION

If you already own older properties, or if you have some low-risk investments with bonds or savings accounts, building new rentals can diversify your investment portfolio. By opting for purpose-built rentals, you're balancing risks and tapping into the potential for passive income generation. As market trends evolve, new builds remain a forward-thinking strategy that can help you protect your assets and continue to generate long-term profits. Additionally, building new allows you to create a sustainable, scalable business model that can support both short-term cash flow and long-term wealth accumulation.

KEY ADVANTAGES OF BUILDING NEW

- **Create your Own Deals:** Tap into markets with this loophole strategy

- **Customization:** You have greater control over the property's design, layout, and features.

- **Purposeful Designs:** Maximize layout efficiency with important features like fire and sound separation, privacy, separate meters, etc.

- **No Inherited Tenants**: Start fresh with a new tenant base, avoiding issues like unhappy tenants and evictions.

- **Higher Returns**: Fewer, higher-value units can lead to greater cash flow and reduced operational costs.

- **More Control Over the Budget:** You can tailor the design of the build to achieve the perfect loan-to-value (LTV) ratio to maximize your profits. A simple design with in-demand features is all you need.

- **Modernization**: Attract high-quality tenants with new, energy-efficient homes that stand out in the market.

- **Lower Maintenance**: New builds mean fewer unexpected repairs and lower long-term maintenance costs.

- **Long-Term Growth**: New construction allows for long-term asset appreciation and increased equity.

- **Diversification**: A new build portfolio can balance risk and increase passive income opportunities.

- **Potential tax benefits**: Depending on your jurisdiction, there may be certain tax incentives or benefits associated with BTR developments. It's advisable to consult with tax professionals to understand the specific tax advantages available in your area.

TOP THREE TAKEAWAYS

1. **Building New Offers More Control and Customization:** New construction gives you the freedom to design properties that meet current market demands. From layout to materials, you can customize everything, maximizing efficiency, privacy, and profitability, without being limited by existing structures or outdated systems.

2. **Higher Returns with Fewer, High-Value Units:** Focusing on new builds allows for higher-value properties, which can provide greater returns per unit. Fewer units with higher value reduce operational costs, simplify management, and increase cash flow compared to older, lower-value properties.

3. **Lower Maintenance and Long-Term Stability:** New construction offers fewer surprises, lower maintenance costs, and a solid foundation for long-term growth. With fewer repairs and more energy-efficient features, you'll attract quality tenants and ensure stable, reliable cash flow over time.

CHAPTER 2

PREPARE YOUR MINDSET, MAKE A PLAN, AND GET STARTED!

Before I dive in, I want to emphasize the importance of having a clear purpose—or a "Why"—behind your real estate investing. Ask yourself, "Why am I doing this?" Simply wanting to make money is not enough. Your "Why" serves as your anchor during turbulent times. Beyond profit, it could mean achieving financial freedom, building a family legacy, or creating a positive impact in your community.

For example, someone's 'Why' might be to generate passive income that allows them the freedom to spend more time with their family. Or, it could be because they've been stuck in the same thankless, soul-sucking job for years, and the only way out is through a different stream of income. This is the kind of 'why' that keeps you grounded when you go through the ups and downs of this business.

Some of you might be starting out and thinking, "I'll just do one deal for now; it won't be too bad for me." Sorry to burst your bubble, but even that one deal will have its share of ups and downs. If it feels too easy, you might have done it wrong! (Joking... kind of.)

Over the years, Rob and I have experienced countless highs and lows as we built our real estate business. Every single deal or project has come with its own unique set of challenges. This journey has taught us invaluable lessons—and given us more gray hairs than we'd like to admit. Yet, working together toward a common goal has also deepened our understanding of and respect for each other.

Being on the same page with your partner and aligning your goals is essential. Just as Rob and I have faced challenges that tested our partnership, many investors struggle to align their visions. This alignment can either strengthen your bond or cause strain. In our case, we've made it a priority to establish shared goals and a clear mission for the business while respecting each other's personal aspirations. Successful partnerships require a balance between shared business objectives and individual priorities. As time goes on, our visions might change or differ from one another, but usually we manage to build compromises and stay on track based on our shared Why.

> TIP: Hold an open and honest discussion with your partner, be it your spouse or whomever you choose to accompany you on this adventure, to determine where you both hope to be in five years' time. Write down your goals and aspirations for your business, including the image you want it to have, its mission statement, the problems it will solve, its target market, and so on. Additionally, you should document each person's individual "Why" for being in the business. Everyone should be ready and willing to work equally hard. You should leave the meeting feeling energized and empowered, like you could move mountains.

UNDERSTAND YOUR GOALS

For years, our primary focus has been on cash flow—the amount of money left after all expenses have been paid. When managed effectively, cash flow can become a primary revenue stream and provide financial freedom. Our goal was to generate enough cash flow to support our lifestyle and break free from traditional nine-to-five jobs. While we've crossed that threshold, I doubt we'll ever fully retire and do nothing—I think we'll always want to work on something meaningful. But moving forward we'll adapt and work smarter instead of harder.

These days, we've started to step back from the day-to-day operations of our business. We've focused on building a capable team and implementing systems that allow the business to run without us being involved in every detail. This shift has given us more freedom while maintaining the momentum of our investments.

Back in 2018, Rob had left his full-time job as an estimator to manage our projects. Even though we hadn't yet hit our monthly cash flow goal, his time was better spent running projects and doing some trade work, saving us significant construction costs. When the projects were completed and refinanced, we always ensured there was enough equity to pay him back while keeping the property cash-flow positive.

As for me, I left a job I loved designing custom homes to take on a less demanding federal government role. It wasn't an easy decision—leaving a dream job is never simple. But the new position was less tasking and time consuming which gave me better work-life balance. Allowing me to support Rob and our business more actively. A part of me was sad to make that decision, but the other part knew that making the change was necessary for us. Sometimes, you have to shuffle things around to align with your long-term goals. We simply kept our eye on the prize and our spirits open to adaptation as we moved through our journey.

Fast forward to now: Our focus has shifted to growing the team and refining processes to scale our business sustainably. Our aim is to fully transition into roles where we oversee operations at a high level, giving us the time and flexibility to explore other passions and opportunities.

HOW TO EFFECTIVELY MANAGE CASH FLOW

Managing cash flow is just as important as generating it. Here are some steps to help you maximize and track it effectively:

1. TRACK EVERY EXPENSE:

Cash flow is not simply the difference between rent and mortgage payments. To calculate it accurately, you must account for all property-related costs, including:

- Mortgage payments (principal and interest)
- Property taxes
- Insurance
- Utilities
- Maintenance and repairs
- Property management fees
- Vacancy rates
- Capital expenditures (e.g., roof replacements, HVAC upgrades)
- Advertising and miscellaneous operating expenses

Create a system to track these expenses regularly—whether through software or a spreadsheet—to avoid surprises.

2. REINVEST SURPLUS:

Any surplus cash flow should be reinvested wisely. This could mean paying down high-interest debt, funding capital improvements, or saving for your next investment. Reinvesting accelerates growth and enhances your portfolio's long-term value.

3. PLAN FOR THE UNEXPECTED:

Always anticipate market shifts or unexpected expenses. Set aside a portion of your cash flow in a reserve fund to cover emergencies like major repairs or prolonged vacancies. A cushion of three to six months' worth of operating expenses is a good starting point.

4. LEVERAGE TECHNOLOGY:

Use property management and accounting software to automate tasks like rent collection, expense tracking, and financial reporting. This ensures accuracy and saves time.

5. MONITOR AND ADJUST:

Cash flow isn't static. Markets change, property values fluctuate, and expenses rise. Regularly review your cash flow, identify trends, and make adjustments as needed.

By following these steps, you can maximize your cash flow and ensure your investments remain sustainable over the long term. Managing cash flow effectively not only supports your lifestyle but also positions you to scale and grow your portfolio strategically.

THE GOALS VS. THE REALITY

Our first goal was to reach $10,000 in monthly cash flow before we turned 30. That equates to a net annual salary of about $60,000 each, or roughly $84,000 gross income in Ontario after accounting for taxes and deductions. The motivation behind this goal was simple: To fund our lifestyles without feeling restricted and to allow us the freedom to travel a few times a year.

Additionally, as our parents grow older, we're increasingly aware of the challenges of government-funded retirement homes in Ontario. Ensuring they receive the best care without relying on those facilities is a significant motivator behind our efforts.

Once we achieved that first 10k milestone, our focus shifted. Instead of targeting a specific dollar amount, our new goal was about achieving a high quality of life by the time we turn 35. This means stepping away from the day-to-day operations of the business and transitioning into the role of distant owners. And we are well on our way there. We are 32 today and already we have a full-time working foreman helping run the builds, a full-time general labour working on the construction sites and doing some property maintenance, a full-time virtual assistant taking care of all things administrative and tenant management, as well as a contract with my mother for turnovers and filling units when needed. We also have a great thing going with a Joint Venture partner on a couple builds that helps alleviate some of the workload and financial strain.

As you can imagine, our cash flow takes a major hit with these hires, but we get a better quality of life out of it. And at a certain point, you *need* to do this. At the least for sanity reasons!

This shift aligns with our efforts to increase automation within the business. If achieving this goal requires reducing cash flow in the short term to invest in support staff and systems, we're more than willing to make that trade-off. Ultimately, it's about building a sustainable business that provides freedom, flexibility, and fulfillment while safeguarding our mental and physical health. Life is already capable of throwing curveballs on its own, we don't need to help it along by adding big stress factors into our lives like choosing to manage large-scale construction projects and 45+ tenants all by ourselves. We should be able to reduce—or even avoid this—with proper systems and great people in place.

HOW WE GOT TO THIS POINT

We were thrilled to hit our first major milestone of $10,000 in monthly cash flow in 2022—the year we turned 30. However, that same year brought new challenges. After navigating a tiring situation with a problematic tenant—while also adjusting to life as first-time parents—we made the decision to hire a property management company.

The tenant had filed a complaint with the Landlord and Tenant Board about construction noise during the day while we worked in the basement unit. He also added that the driveway hadn't been paved—this, during the *first year* of the building's construction. Appearing in front of the board while sleep-deprived and caring for a newborn was exhausting.

On top of that, he took to every local Facebook group he could find, posting defamation posts about us and our company—even though he had already moved out months earlier. Which was pointless—there was no money owed on either side, and nothing left for him to gain. Why he felt the need to go out of his way to play these games was beyond us. It was nothing more than an annoyance. Like a mosquito that won't land— just keeps buzzing around you. Pointless, irritating, and something you want to swat away.

We found his new address and hired a lawyer to send him a cease and desist letter for defamation. He stopped posting online and also lost his case at the board. The whole ordeal was stupid. All we lost was our precious time—and for what? Still, the experience proved something important: we had outgrown these insignificant situations.

We had bigger, more meaningful goals to focus on—like continuing to scale while protecting our family time. It was time to outsource tenant management and move forward.

We were initially hesitant to hire a PM because we knew this decision would reduce our cash flow. After finally hitting our goal, it felt like a step backward. But it revealed a critical oversight in our planning: We hadn't accounted for management expenses in our cash flow calculations. Whether you hire in-house staff or outsource, management costs should be part of your budget from the start. Properly planning for these "growing pains" is essential because you can't scale effectively if you're trying to manage everything yourself.

I know many of you self-manage and even fully omit management fees from your cash flow calculations to make the numbers look better. Just remember, at some point, you will need to bring in help, and it's better to plan for it now.

Later that year, despite taking a hit in our cash flow goals, we decided I wouldn't return to my government job after my maternity leave. Instead, I focused on the business alongside Rob, prioritizing family time and concentrating on big-picture strategies rather than spreading myself too thin.

However, less than a year later, interest rates rose drastically, and we had three mortgages coming up for renewal in 2023. The average rate jumped from three percent to six percent, adding pressure on our cash flow. Thankfully, we'd anticipated this possibility. By studying market cycles, the history and the drivers that make up these market shifts, we understood what would happen and knew we would find ways to adapt. We had analyzed our portfolio and determined we had been conservative enough in all our builds. We had enough equity to sustain wavering shifts in the market.

When the time came, two out of three of the properties had enough cash flow to sustain the increase. Tenant turnovers also allowed us to raise rents, restoring cash flow to pre-renewal levels. For the third property, we got creative and converted it from duplex to a triplex, significantly boosting income (see Chapter 10 for more details on one of the coolest projects we've done).

We restructured by letting go of our property manager and hiring a part-time virtual assistant (VA). Once we had efficient processes in place, managing our units became a minimal time investment. By hiring a VA instead of a full-time property manager, we saved thousands each month. For instance, with a portfolio generating $50,000 in gross monthly income, even an eight percent management fee would cost $4,000. By comparison, we spent roughly $2,500 per month hiring a VA for 16 hours a week and $1,000 annually investing in management software. Even as your portfolio income grows, the PM fee would grow with it, but the cost of the VA could be capped. Although you should consider giving annual raises to your VA or increase their hours when needed, the cost growth is still a lot slower than the PM percentage fee. I talk more about hiring a VA in Chapter 16.

Turns out, when necessary, you find ways to make things work. Significant changes can feel daunting, but they often signal growth and opportunity. While growing pains are uncomfortable, they're also exciting chances to adjust and improve. Today, our VA works full time for us. Plus we put my mom in charge of doing showings and finding tenants when needed since our VA is not local and couldn't do that part. We've since gained a better focus on our family life, and the long-term vision for our business, and we continue to refine our systems as we pursue our objectives.

TIP: Before leaving your job, ensure you have consistent cash flow and sufficient savings. Aim for at least a year of steady cash flow to handle any unexpected maintenance expenses without derailing your finances. It's also crucial to maintain cash reserves. Selling underperforming properties to reinvest in higher-yielding ones can provide both financial stability and peace of mind as you transition away from a steady paycheck.

MOM-PRENEURSHIP

Leaving my government job in 2022 felt like the right move. I hoped it would bring relief and more free time. But as a new mom and an entrepreneur, I quickly learned that "more free time" was wishful thinking. Balancing motherhood with running a construction and rental business was tougher than any job I'd ever had.

Even in the beginning when we had just hired a property manager to handle tenants, the construction side of the business remained demanding. Between designs, pre-permit coordination, material selection, bookkeeping, and accounts payable, my plate was overflowing. I also handled tenant placements myself to avoid paying the one-month rent fee charged by the PM.

I knew motherhood would be time-consuming and exhausting, but I didn't anticipate the absolutely overwhelming sense of failure I'd feel daily. Before becoming a mom, I had spent eight years focused solely on growing our business. Afterward, I felt like I couldn't give 100 percent to anything—not the business, my health, my child, nor the household duties. I was constantly pulled in every direction, ending most days feeling conflicted and defeated.

One incident stands out. Our son was five months old, and I was sitting on the floor with him while trying to respond to emails from that difficult tenant. Sleep-deprived and frustrated, I snapped at my son for needing my attention. The look on his face broke my heart. That night, I told Rob we were hiring a property manager, no matter the cost.

Fast forward to 2024: after revamping our systems, letting go of the property manager, and hiring a VA—even just for 16 hours a week—everything shifted. That VA took all the tedious tasks off my plate, and having help with the administrative side of the construction business felt like a game changer. Still, I carried all the big-picture responsibilities my VA couldn't handle.

By then, our son was going to daycare three days a week. We had chosen that intentionally—to give him a hybrid lifestyle and to be present during these precious preschool years. And yet, I was still struggling. No matter how much help I brought in, I realized that unless I was disciplined and intentional with my time, I'd always feel like I was falling short.

Most entrepreneurs are accomplishment junkies—I know *we* are. As soon as we finished a project, we'd dive into a new one. Not just because we wanted to, but because we still hadn't achieved certain goals. You come to a point where if you stop growing your portfolio too early, you don't have enough cashflow to support full time help so you need to keep managing yourself, yet you can't keep growing all by yourself either so you need to hire to grow but you need to grow to hire… get my drift?

Anyway, eventually, I read a few books and listened to podcasts that helped me rethink my approach on time management. Brandon Turner often talks about time blocking on *The Better Life Podcast*, and the book *10x is Easier than 2x* by Dan Sullivan introduced me to the concepts of Focus Days, Buffer Days, and Rest Days.

Adopting time-blocking strategies has been a game-changer. I structured my week into these three types of days to balance work and family life. On Focus Days, when my son was at daycare, I tackled high-priority tasks. I organized these tasks the day before so I didn't waste time, and from 8:30 a.m. to 3:45 p.m., I worked exclusively on them with phone notifications silenced. I reserved an hour or so during this time to eat, exercise, and return urgent calls.

Buffer Days were lighter workdays when my son was home. I might answer a few emails and calls, but those days were mainly for chores and spending one-on-one time with him. Finally, weekends were Rest Days.

I still use this system whenever I need it. I focus on what I can accomplish with the time I have, and at the end of the day, I make a conscious effort to reflect on the progress I've made instead of fixating on what's left to do. That simple mindset shift allows me to feel pride and contentment, even if my wins are small.

It's easy for parents to fall into the trap of trying to be a Super-Parent, Super-Spouse, and Super-Preneur all at once. But we can't forget to put ourselves first. If you're time-blocking correctly, you're doing just that—scheduling time not only for your family and what matters most but also for yourself and your health. For me, this is the only way I've discovered to feel like I'm being the best version of myself.

START RIGHT – HAVE A BUSINESS PLAN

I think having a written business plan helps, especially when applying for financing to build your first property. Take the time to look this over, I'll even let you use our plan as a template to make it easy for you to create your own. Most lenders will not require this document, but adding it may improve your chances of approval, especially with private lenders. This is because it shows that you are prepared, and have done your homework. Even if you don't use it to apply for lending, having one written before diving in helps get your mindset in the right direction.

So, what is a business plan exactly? At its core, it's a document that outlines what your business is, how it operates, and where it's headed. It paints a picture of your goals, your strategy, and how you plan to get there. While lenders sometimes ask for it, many business owners write one for themselves—it helps track progress, clarify direction, and make better decisions as things evolve. Your plan might include things like the story behind your business, your target market, the way your business runs day-to-day, who's involved, and your financial outlook.

There's no one-size-fits-all, and it doesn't have to be perfect or 20 pages long. What matters is that it reflects your vision and helps guide your next steps.

I still remember the night Rob and I sat down to write our first business plan—if you could even call it that. It was little more than a page ripped from a notebook, filled with scribbled goals jotted down in no particular order. As we reviewed our chaotic notes, we began discussing our vision: Where we wanted our business to be in five years, the types of properties we hoped to invest in, and the lifestyle we aimed to achieve. It wasn't just about financial success; it was about building a life that allowed us to spend more time with family, support our parents as they aged, and perhaps help our nieces and nephew financially with their education in the future.

Eventually, we graduated from that scrap of paper to a digital document, though this upgrade only happened under pressure: The one bank we had been working with pulled out of a deal at the last minute, leaving us scrambling to secure a private loan. We had applied with the usual revenue documents and had even received verbal confirmation from the bank. But just as we were about to pick up our $40,000 permit, they backed out.

The timing couldn't have been worse. We had already excavated the site and were managing spring water seepage while waiting for the permit. In a panic, we called our accountant, who also happened to be a friend. He made a few calls and connected us with private lenders through his network. He even arranged a meeting in the same week.

We knew we had to present ourselves professionally, and a proper business plan was critical. In a rush, I pulled together a document in just one day. Looking back, I wish I had prepared it sooner. A few days later, the bank came back to us, admitting they'd made a mistake in their calculations and were willing to proceed. But it was too late—we decided to stick with the private lender, even at a higher interest rate (9 percent compared to four percent), to establish a relationship and build our reputation as we realized that relying on a single source of financing wasn't sustainable.

Later, we learned that the business plan I'd hastily created played a significant role in sealing the deal with the private lender, as well as securing a nine percent interest vs a higher one. It wasn't anything fancy—just a Word document that included details and photos of the properties in our portfolio at the time, a brief summary of who we were, our goals, and an attached Excel sheet showing our finances.

That's the essence of a business plan. It's simply a structured and professional way to combine three key elements: Your goals, your financials, and your portfolio.

Since then, I've reworked the layout of our business plan more professionally for the sake of sharing it with you, so that you had something of better quality to present to investors than what we had.

⬇ You can find a copy of it through our 'Free Toolkit' download on our website www.thenewbuildcouple.com.

Here's an overview of the plan. It includes:

- a title page,
- table of contents,

- company overview,
- business description,
- portfolio overview,
- market analysis,
- operating plan,
- roles and responsibilities, SOPs
- compliance and continuing education
- marketing and sales plan,
- financial plan,
- risk mitigation,
- and an appendix of our portfolio's financial health.

Some of my sensitive information has been blocked out or removed altogether.

When drafting your business plan, be honest about your strengths and weaknesses. A realistic assessment will help you identify areas where you need support or additional training. Also, revisit and revise your plan regularly as your business grows and your goals evolve.

A FEW DOS AND DON'TS OF WRITING A BUSINESS PLAN:

DOS:

- Provide necessary details but be concise
  - ↳ Try to answer basic key questions about the business like who, where, when, how, what, why and how much
- Take the time to do your research before writing the plan
  - ↳ For example, the research on the market you plan to invest in
- Provide supporting data for statements
  - ↳ Don't make assertions based on speculation or a gut feeling. Back it up with well-documented data from reliable sources.

- Preferably use 3rd person (no "I" statements)
  - ↳ For example, instead of "I will reach out to other investors in this market…" write "ABC Properties will reach out to investors in this market…"
- Tailor the plan to your audience
  - ↳ Keep the reader in mind as well as the reason why this person is looking at your plan. You can adjust the plan and the purpose of it if your audience changes.
- Review and adjust plan periodically as your business evolves

DON'TS:

- Don't over promise, keep it realistic
  - ↳ Don't be overly ambitious when describing the business and the goals. Yes, you should be promoting it, but you should also be able to justify more realistic outcomes.
- Don't hide shortcomings, provide mitigations
  - ↳ No business is perfect, the key is to show how the business is equipped to persevere in hard times and in good.
- Don't over or under describe – information should be provided in adequate detail
  - ↳ If you're not clear on the goals or if you write it feeling rushed, the end result will show
- Don't use industry jargon – keep it simple and explain any acronyms when first presented

Since business plans are often presented for financing, lenders, financiers and potential investors are often the target audience, but they can also be used beyond a need for financing. You can use them for transitioning in new employees. Let's say you hire a new junior property manager to help with tenant management, you could provide a copy of the business plan as part of their initiation so that they can better understand your business and the role they will play in helping to grow it.

Bonus note: I strongly recommend also having a Standard Operating Procedures document (SOPs) for this exact scenario. It would facilitate your new employee training a whole lot and will help business to run as a well-oiled machine. SOPs ensure that tasks are performed the same way every time, regardless of who does them. They increase quality of work and efficiency by providing clear guidelines for tasks and processes. They help maintain compliance, and reduce risks. SOPs are vital for training, accountability, and sustaining operational continuity in any business. I talk more about SOPs in Chapter 16, and I would recommend reading *Traction* by Gino Wickman.

TOP THREE TAKEAWAYS:

1. **Define Your "Why"**: Having a clear and compelling reason for investing in real estate is crucial. This purpose will keep you motivated through the highs and lows of the journey.

2. **Align Goals with Your Partner**: Ensure you and your partner are on the same page by having open discussions about your goals and aspirations. Documenting these goals can help you stay aligned and motivated.

3. **Plan for Success**: Having a well-crafted business plan is crucial for demonstrating your seriousness and preparedness, especially when seeking financing.

CHAPTER 3

SELECTING THE RIGHT MARKET

Now that you understand the benefits of Build to Rent and you're ready to get started, you might be wondering: *Can I even do this in my market?* I get this question all the time—especially because my audience is about half Canadian and half American. So let's break down some of the major differences between the two countries and, more importantly, whether this strategy still works in both.

U.S. VS. CANADA: IS ONE MARKET EASIER?

HOME PRICES VS. HOUSEHOLD INCOME (AFFORDABILITY)

In May 2024, the average home price in Canada was around CAD $750,000, while in the U.S. it was approximately USD $430,000. Now let's compare that to income:

- Median after-tax income in Canada (2022): CAD $70,500
- Median household income in the U.S. (2022): USD $74,580

If you do the math, that's a home price-to-income ratio of 10.6x in Canada, and 5.8x in the U.S.—nearly half. That means real estate in Canada is generally much less affordable, even before you factor in higher taxes and construction costs.

NEW CONSTRUCTION & APPROVAL PROCESSES

Canada's approval process for new builds is often slower and more bureaucratic—especially in urban areas. Zoning changes and environmental assessment requirements can take months, if not years. In contrast, many parts of the U.S. (especially in the Sunbelt) have fast-tracked development approvals to keep up with demand. This gives American investors a leg up when it comes to speed-to-market. Although Canada is also trying to fast-track things, I have yet to truly experience it. Currently, provincial laws are written vaguely, leaving municipalities to interpret them any way they please. Creating chaos, confusion, and even more delays.

CONSTRUCTION COSTS & MATERIALS

Canada typically faces higher costs for materials, labor, and transportation—driven by a smaller population, less competition among trades, and longer winters. In many U.S. regions, it's not only cheaper to build, but trades are more available and pricing is more competitive, which directly impacts ROI.

POPULATION GROWTH & DEMAND

Both countries are growing, but growth looks different. Canada has a housing supply shortage that isn't being solved fast enough, especially in Ontario and BC. Meanwhile, U.S. states like Texas, Florida, and Arizona are seeing massive migration and job creation—fueling steady demand *and* new development. In both countries, the need for rental housing is very real.

FINANCING & MORTGAGE STRUCTURES

Canada's mortgage structure usually involves 5-year fixed terms with 25–30 year amortizations. This creates renewal risk if rates rise. The U.S. offers more predictability with 30-year fixed mortgages, which is a big plus for long-term investors. Also, U.S. homeowners can deduct mortgage interest on their primary residence—Canadians can't (though rental property interest is deductible in both countries).

SO... DOES BUILD TO RENT STILL WORK IN BOTH COUNTRIES?

Yes—absolutely. But the path looks a bit different.

In the U.S., investors often have an easier time scaling. Between more affordable prices, friendlier financing, and faster development processes, you can get a project up and running faster—especially in high-growth states. Not to mention the fact that the U.S. has the possibility of 1031 exchanges, and Canada does not… womp womp.

In Canada, the barriers are higher. Costs are steeper, and regulations are more intense. But here's the truth: if we've been able to make it work in Canada—despite all that—you can make it work wherever you are.

We started from scratch in what I'd call an averagely expensive and regulated market. We learned to navigate the red tape, manage rising costs, and still produce strong returns. So if you're in a more affordable or investor-friendly region, you might even find it easier to succeed.

That's the beauty of this strategy: it's adaptable. Whether you're building in Ontario or Oklahoma, Alberta or Arizona—there's a way in.

WHICH TYPE OF MARKET FAVORS BUILD-TO-RENT?

While this strategy can be implemented almost everywhere, you need to find a location where the property values are higher than the building costs. You don't want to be building in a market with lower-than-average home prices, where the building cost may exceed the property's value. If you are in a market where you can buy a home for $100,000, building from scratch is likely going to cost more, and, therefore, you wouldn't be in the right market to implement this strategy. You need to fully understand the local market and its characteristics, which will include factors such as supply and demand and employment levels, for example. You will also need to understand market trends and cycles, and how they affect the local market.

During the Covid-19 pandemic, the housing market saw a rapid increase in value, prompting many to invest in new builds. However, we advised caution due to the potential effects of this kind of rapid inflation. I called it fake inflation. At the time, the cost of goods and services was at an all-time high as well. Although home values were still higher than construction costs, the narrowing gap made the market for new builds increasingly risky. We anticipated that if values declined with rising interest rates, the cost-value gap could disappear altogether. This concern is now manifesting with the 2023 rate hikes, as those who built or bought homes at high prices during the pandemic are seeing their property values drop, potentially erasing any existing equity.

When building a property to hold long-term, focusing on your costs and mortgage payments is essential, as they will have a larger impact than fluctuating values and interest rates. We still built during the pandemic but we were more careful about not relying on appreciation to continue spiking upward. Instead, we balanced our budget by subbing out less to trades and using our in-house team for most of the labor — a.k.a. Rob and a full time helper. The goal was to keep our loan-to-value (LTV) ratio within a 70 percent comfort zone. From the start, we also budgeted for a higher interest rate, as we knew from historic interest rate cycles that those all-time low rates were unlikely to last.

> 📄 NOTE: An LTV ratio means the loan amount compared to the value of the property. For easy math, if the property is worth 100,000$ but you're getting a loan for 80,000$, that's an LTV ratio of 80 percent.

Turns out we were right. By the time construction was complete, we were stuck locking in a 6.03 percent interest rate for three years where rates had been at two percent only eight months earlier. Thankfully though, we had managed to keep our LTV ratio at 63 percent, which still allowed for positive cash flow. It's always best to plan for a worst-case scenario. Effective planning starts from doing proper market research to know how the odds are stacked for or against you.

MARKET RESEARCH

When building to rent, choosing your location is one of the most critical factors. Look for urban centers or areas with high population growth and limited housing supply. These markets often have strong and consistent rental demand, ensuring high occupancy rates and steady cash flow. Neighborhoods with good schools, public transportation, and access to employment centers tend to attract long-term tenants, making them ideal for BTR projects.

This framework applies not only to new builds but to real estate investing in general. Below is the step-by-step process we use every time we evaluate a new area—including where to find the data.

TIP: Investors often get caught up in the purchase price alone. But a high-priced property in a growing market can outperform a "cheap" one in a stagnant town. Focus on long-term fundamentals like demand, policies, and your ability to build efficiently and rent quickly.

NOTE: The sources listed below for where to find market data are Canadian-specific. Since I'm based in Canada and have built my portfolio here, these are the tools and resources I'm most familiar with. If you're investing in the U.S. or elsewhere, I encourage you to seek out equivalent local sources—but I won't pretend to be an expert in markets I haven't personally worked in.

1. RESEARCH THE LOCAL ECONOMY

Look for: Unemployment rates, job growth, industry strength. A strong local economy can lead to higher demand for real estate and potentially higher property values.

Where to find it:

- Statistics Canada or local municipality websites
- Economic Development offices (to find an Economic Development Office, search the name of the city or town followed by "Economic Development Office" or "Economic Development Department" (e.g., "Orillia Economic Development Office"). This will usually lead you to a municipal webpage with reports, contacts, and resources. In smaller towns, if no official office exists, contact the City Clerk's Office or Planning Department— they can direct you to the right person.)
- News articles about new employers moving in

Look for regions with job diversity and growing employment opportunities, not just one dominant industry. Areas near new warehouses, hospitals, or tech hubs often signal future growth.

2. ANALYZE POPULATION GROWTH

Look for: Consistent population increases over 5–10 years.
Where to find it:

- Statistics Canada census data
- Local municipal planning reports
- School enrollment data (indirect growth indicator)

Population growth usually leads to higher housing demand. Bonus points if housing supply is lagging behind demand—this creates upward pressure on rents.

3. EVALUATE PROPERTY VALUES

Look for: Historical price appreciation and price-per-square-foot data
Where to find it:

- MLS sales data (ask a local realtor or use Realtor.ca sold listings)
- HouseSigma, Zolo, or Zoocasa

You want to see steady, sustainable appreciation. Sharp spikes can indicate bubbles. Look for areas where you can build below resale value, which gives you equity on day one.

4. CHECK RENTAL RATES AND VACANCY

Look for: Strong average rents, low vacancy (<5%)
Where to find it:

- Rentals.ca, Zumper, or Facebook marketplace
- Ask local property managers or realtors
- CMHC Rental Market Reports

Compare your estimated rents to build costs. Ensure there's enough cash flow to support your financing and operating expenses—even with interest rate increases or short vacancies.

5. UNDERSTAND LOCAL REGULATIONS

Look for: Favourable zoning, fast permitting, pro-density attitudes
Where to find it:

- City planning department or municipal website
- Zoning bylaw documents and Official Plans (OP)
- Phone call or in-person visit with a planner or building department

Find out: Is the city encouraging new housing, or do they make it hard to build? Is your project allowed "as of right" or will you need rezoning or variances?

6. ASSESS THE COMPETITION

Look for: How your planned build compares to current listings
Where to find it:

- Rentals.ca, Facebook Marketplace, Kijiji (for rentals)
- Realtor.ca, HouseSigma (for resale comparisons)

- In-person visits to open houses or nearby buildings

This helps you see how your finishes, layouts, and unit sizes stack up. You'll spot gaps—like a market full of outdated 2-bed units with no 3-bed options.

7. TALK TO LOCAL EXPERTS

Look for: Real-world insight from those active in the area
Where to find it:

- Realtors who work with investors
- City staff in planning, permits, or economic development
- Property managers and landlords
- Facebook groups or real estate investor meetups

Ask what areas are heating up, where delays happen, and what tenant profiles look like. These conversations will reveal things no spreadsheet ever could.

> TIP: Always double-check online data with someone who actually works in the area. Local insights are often the difference between a good project and a great one.

Remember that every market and investor's circumstances are different. Before implementing the BTR strategy, do your research, consider your financial situation and risk appetite, and make sure you clearly understand the financing that is needed. Building a property from scratch can be more complex than buying and renovating, so you must be prepared.

> Download your free printable Market Research Worksheet at www.thenewbuildcouple.com

UNDERSTANDING MARKET CYCLES

While timing the market perfectly is nearly impossible, being well-informed about market cycles, economic conditions, and tenant demand can help you make better investment decisions. Luckily, the real estate market, much like the economy, operates in cycles. While the specific timing of these cycles can be difficult to predict, understanding their patterns allows investors to make informed decisions about when to build, buy, or sell. In his book *The Secrets to the Canadian Real Estate Cycle*, Don Campbell explains that real estate markets generally pass through four phases: **Boom**, **Slump**, **Recovery**, and **Peak**. While this book focuses on Canada, these patterns hold true in many developed markets.

The **Boom** phase is characterized by rapidly rising property values and high demand. This is a time when investors tend to get aggressive, purchasing properties to flip or taking on significant leverage. However, even though this phase may seem like an ideal time to invest, it's important to exercise caution. Property values can rise quickly, but if you're not careful, you may buy at the market's peak, limiting your potential returns. During the boom, demand for rentals also surges as people flock to areas with job growth or development.

Conversely, the **Slump** phase can be an excellent time for long-term investors. Property values decline, and sellers may become more motivated to offload their assets at discounted prices. This phase is less competitive, and you have time to negotiate favorable terms. The slump is a great time to start new BTR projects because construction costs may also decrease. During a slump, demand for rental properties remains strong, as fewer people are buying homes and instead turn to renting.

The **Recovery** phase follows the slump and is a transitional period where property values and rental rates begin to rise again. Investors can capitalize on the recovery by purchasing properties with strong appreciation potential. If you're building to rent, this is an opportune time to lock in financing, as interest rates may start to decrease in anticipation of renewed economic activity. Keep in mind that rental markets tend to stabilize during the recovery, which can improve your property's cash flow as vacancy rates decline and rental rates inch upward.

Finally, the **Peak** phase is the highest point of the cycle, marked by market saturation. Investors may need to focus on maintaining their current portfolio and avoiding aggressive expansion, as prices are at their highest, and growth is slowing. Even during this phase, however, BTR projects can thrive because housing affordability becomes an issue, and many people will opt to rent instead of buying at inflated prices.

APPLYING MARKET CYCLES TO BUILD-TO-RENT

Building to Rent is a versatile strategy that can work across all phases of the real estate cycle. During the boom, rising property values and high demand for housing gives landlords the opportunity to charge premium rents. However, be cautious about over-leveraging during this phase, as a market correction could negatively impact your returns if you don't have a financial cushion.

During Covid, a lot of newbie builders decided to build rental properties while it was easier to get access to cheap credit. The sharp rise in costs of everything left them with a big mortgage, but the extremely low variable rates made up for it. It was fine while rents were also high. As soon as the interest rates spiked though (the correction), they found themselves in a negative cashflow situation. Tenant turnovers proved to be more difficult at maintaining their high rents.

In the **Slump**, when property values decrease and fewer buyers are in the market, BTR projects provide a steady income stream. During economic slowdowns, more people rent due to tighter lending standards and job insecurity. But it usually means that current tenants stay put longer, making it harder to find great tenants since there aren't a lot of turnovers happening.

Construction costs tend to be lower during slumps, which can reduce the upfront cost of your project, allowing for better profit margins in the long run. 2024 was a slump year in our market, and although our construction budgets were fantastic during our builds, we found it was harder to find great tenants and increase rents.

As the market enters the **Recovery** phase, rental demand typically remains robust, and you'll see gradual increases in rental rates. This is a perfect time to capitalize on market growth, as your properties may appreciate, and financing becomes more accessible. Projects started during the recovery phase can benefit from both rising rental income and increasing property values.

The **Peak** phase poses unique challenges but also offers opportunities for BTR investors. While it may not be the best time to start new projects due to high land and material costs, rental demand often remains strong as housing prices soar beyond the reach of many potential buyers. During this phase, it's crucial to ensure your properties are well-maintained and competitively priced to secure tenants.

STRATEGIC CONSIDERATIONS FOR BUILDING TO RENT

Half of our portfolio is located in rural suburbs about 30 minutes from a major city, but just 10 to 15 minutes from a smaller, fast-growing township where the rest of our properties are. These areas rent extremely well and generate solid cash flow. One reason is that there's often less competition for new construction rentals in more rural or secondary markets. Many renters still value quiet, country-like settings that remain within easy reach of major amenities. As long as the community is growing, has good schools, and offers a peaceful neighborhood feel—while staying accessible to a larger city—it can be a great area to invest in. Just remember: your build costs must stay in line with the final appraised value to make the numbers work.

It's essential to maintain continuous market research throughout the life of your project. Real estate markets change, tenant preferences evolve, and economic conditions shift, so keeping a close eye on these factors will help you adapt your strategy as needed. Look at tenant demographics and adjust the features or amenities you offer to meet their needs. For instance, families may value proximity to good schools, while young professionals may prefer access to public transportation or nightlife.

A prime example of shifting factors occurred during the construction of one of our triplexes in a sought-after urban area. Just before the new school year began, the local school system altered its bus routes, increasing the minimum distance for pickup. As a result, many families discovered that their children's bus service had been canceled, requiring them to walk longer distances in freezing winter conditions and cross busy streets during peak traffic hours. Our triplex, which had been within the original bus route radius and designed with three-bedroom units to attract families, suddenly became less appealing to parents concerned about their children's safety. Located on one side of a main street, with all local schools on the other, the property's desirability decreased for young families. While our only recourse would have been to file a complaint with the mayor—which would have been useless—it serves as a clear example of how unforeseen changes can impact a project's appeal.

Building to Rent projects should also focus on quality and amenities. Offering high-quality construction and desirable amenities—such as modern appliances, energy-efficient designs, and communal spaces— makes your properties more attractive to tenants. This can lead to lower vacancy rates and higher rent premiums. However, it's important to strike a balance between adding features and staying within budget, as over-investing in amenities that don't offer a strong return on investment could eat into your profits.

Selecting the right market is one of the most important decisions you'll make in a Build to Rent strategy. It can determine not just your rental demand, but your long-term equity growth, tenant profile, and even your ability to scale. Whether you're targeting a booming suburb, a transitional neighborhood, or a quiet rural township with growth potential, the key is to anchor your decisions in solid research—not assumptions.

Don't just follow the hype or build where land is cheapest. Dig into local economic indicators, understand population trends, explore employment anchors, and look at upcoming developments or infrastructure projects. Surround yourself with local knowledge—from economic development offices to realtors and municipal planners—and compare multiple locations before pulling the trigger.

At the end of the day, smart market selection creates a strong foundation for everything that follows in your Build to Rent journey. It's not just about where people want to live today—but where they'll still want to live five, ten, or twenty years from now.

TOP THREE TAKEAWAYS:

1. **Importance of Market Understanding**: To effectively implement the Build and Hold Strategy, it's crucial to understand the local market, including property values, building costs, and economic conditions. Investing in areas where property values are higher than building costs ensures profitability.

2. **Market Cycles and Strategic Timing**: Recognizing market cycles—boom, slump, recovery, and peak—enables investors to tailor their strategies accordingly. For instance, building to rent can be advantageous in each phase, offering stability in slumps and capitalizing on high demand during booms and peaks.

3. **Thorough Market Research**: Conducting detailed market research is essential for informed decision-making. This includes analyzing local economic health, population growth, property values, rental rates, regulations, and competitive landscapes. Engaging local experts and staying informed about economic fundamentals are also key to success.

CHAPTER 4

GETTING STARTED

You might be tempted to jump straight into a medium-to-large multi-unit build (5+ units), but speaking from experience, traditional financing for this type of project may not even be possible. Your starting point will depend heavily on your financial profile and what you can get pre-approved for at the bank.

A larger build as a first time build may only be feasible if you're an experienced investor, partnering with someone else, or in an exceptionally strong financial position — and even then, restrictions can still apply.

For now, I'm going to focus on the average person getting started at a slower pace with the goal of securing traditional financing for a smaller project (4 units or fewer).

If banks are saying no even for 4 units or less, don't walk away from the strategy altogether. Instead, consider revisiting it with an even smaller-scale build in mind — like a single-unit or duplex — since these typically involve lower loan values and less risk for lenders.

But make sure you have a Plan B in place. Let me explain what that could look like — and remember, this is just to get your foot in the door of the BTR world.

When we first started, we focused on single-family homes even though it wasn't entirely by choice. Our initial intention was to build an up-and-down duplex for our first real investment property (following the build of our own home). However, securing financing for the duplex was challenging due to insufficient funds for the down payment. As a result, we adjusted our plans and obtained approval to construct a single-family home that fell within our pre-approved loan budget. We leveraged the home equity line of credit (HELOC)* from our primary home for the down payment on this new one. But, in implementing our Plan B, we carefully planned the layout and structure in a way that we could easily convert it into a duplex later. We did this by strategically planning our stairs to the basement and adding in a "side" door via those stairs. All we needed to do was put a wall up between the stairs that led to the basement and the main floor, and we had our secondary unit ready to go.

> TIP: A HELOC is a type of loan that allows homeowners to borrow against the equity in their home. It is a revolving line of credit, meaning that the borrower can draw on the line of credit as needed, up to a specified limit, and pay back the borrowed amount with interest at any given time. HELOCs typically have a variable interest rate and can be used for expenses, such as home renovations or debt consolidation.

Let's nickname this project "The Training Wheels Project," symbolizing its potential to serve as an example of a stepping stone toward more ambitious ventures in the future. After completing the Training Wheels Project, we rented out the entire house, including the unfinished basement, for $1,500/month. I don't remember our expenses back then between the mortgage and everything, but I do remember just barely breaking even.

Given how well construction went, we decided to build another single-family home the following year, and then another. However, we soon realized that our long-term profit strategy was flawed. Tenants tend to become very comfortable in single-family homes and stay for extended periods. You would think this would be a good thing, but it's extremely difficult to increase rent prices in Ontario during a tenancy. You can only increase by the yearly maximum set by the province which historically has never been more than 2.5 percent, unless the property was built after November 15, 2018. And these were all built between 2016 and early 2018.

The only way to keep up with a positive cashflow, increasing taxes and interest rates, is by having new tenants every couple of years in order to reset to a new rent price. And mathematically, it just makes more sense to have multiple rents under one roof to support all expenses and achieve a much more profitable cashflow every single month.

In 2018, the tenants living in the Training Wheels Project gave us notice that they needed to move out. Only two years had passed since its original construction, and the time had come to convert it into our intended duplex. With just a weekend's worth of work, we were able to close off the main floor from the basement. Luckily, rental rates had increased significantly in just those two years. We found a tenant to occupy the main floor right away for $1,300/month. The basement unit, after a three-month renovation, rented for $1,150/month. In total, we increased the gross income of this property by $950/month and were able to refinance with its added value to pull out $75,000 to reinvest in a new project.

Currently, as of 2025, the top unit of the Training Wheels Project rents for $1,925/month and the basement unit for $1,328/month (although the basement is worth about 1,500-1,600$ if it weren't rent controlled). If the home were still a single unit today, the full home might rent for $2,500/month. The impact that extra units under one roof can have on your cash flow is significant. It did not take us long to sell the other single family homes that we had built and to focus exclusively on multi-unit builds. Especially since new legislation removed rent control on new builds after November 15, 2018.

We concentrated on selling these homes while values were soaring. We reinvested the capital from the sales profits into new projects and paid down the mortgage on our personal home to use the larger HELOC as a temporary tool during our builds. Our HELOC also serves as a quick way to secure land deals while we work out favourable financing terms with lenders.

In conclusion, we could have given up when the bank initially denied our approval for financing the duplex, but the fact that we proceeded anyway gave us significant advantages. We bolstered our ability to obtain construction loans by adding a second constructed property to our portfolio, which established a history and relationship of trust with our lender. It increased our overall equity and borrowing capability. It was a way of propelling ourselves into the world of real estate investing.

Truthfully, what to start with depends on your financial situation. If you lack the down payment, as we did, then obtaining approval for a smaller loan and beginning with a single-family home or a duplex may be a good first step. Especially now that there are new incentives by the government to densify existing zonings, like adding a second unit to a single family or a third unit to a duplex (I'll talk more about this in Chapter 10). Bottom line, multi-unit builds are usually the main goal as they offer considerable benefits over single-family homes, such as steady cash flow, expenses spread out over multiple units, and faster scalability.

> NOTE: The plans for The Training Wheels Project are available for purchase on our website www.thenewbuildcouple.com. It's a small rectangular shaped building that fits on almost any lot.

LESSONS LEARNED DURING OUR FIRST REAL DEAL

1. You don't need all the answers before starting to invest; sometimes it's best to just get started and figure out the answers as you go.

2. Getting financing for the first deal can be more challenging than you'd expect. Expect the worst, don't give up and keep working through the weeds until you find a solution.

3. Every roadblock that seems like a dead end is usually just a detour, because there's always another route you can take.

4. Keep emotions in check. There's no room for them in business. It's all about facts, numbers, rules and contracts.

5. Expect the Unexpected. Be prepared for unexpected costs, unplanned work, delays, disagreements and unpleasantness. Stay calm, deal with the issue, adjust the course and keep grinding.

6. You're going to work long hours. You will feel overwhelmed, and you ~~may~~ will cry.

7. You can't hire for everything on the first deal, nor should you. The first deal is about learning all the ropes. It's important to know how everything gets done so you can fully understand your business inside and out, to properly delegate later.

8. Understand true cashflow. Don't just assume that cashflow means rental income minus mortgage, insurance and taxes. Include all the hidden expenses: Maintenance, cap ex, vacancy, management, etc.

9. Understand legal and regulatory requirements: Familiarize yourself with local laws and regulations related to property ownership, rental agreements, and tenant rights. Don't go in blindly, because the early mistakes of not knowing can cost you the most.

10. Create an exit strategy. Can you easily sell the property or change its purpose to short term or commercial leasing if needed? Like with our Training wheels project, we knew we could easily convert to a duplex for more cashflow. We could easily convert it back to a single family and sell it to someone who wants a versatile property.

11. Patience and long-term perspective: Manage expectations and patience. Real estate investing often requires patience and a long-term perspective to see significant returns.

12. Yet, also expect to be *hooked* after your first deal. Real estate investing is like a drug. You'll want to do more.

COMMON MISTAKES TO AVOID

It's no secret that having prior construction experience can provide a significant advantage, but even without experience, success is possible with the right guidance. While I don't recommend jumping into a project without knowledge, a good mentor can make all the difference. When we began our first build, we were complete newbies. Luckily, my parent's experience offered us invaluable support. If you don't have someone like that, reach out to contractors for guidance—sometimes paying for their expertise is well worth the investment.

Alternatively, gaining hands-on experience by working with a construction company can be incredibly valuable. Ideally, you would want to work for a company that builds for investment purposes, similar to ours. This way, you not only learn about construction but also gain insight into real estate investing. One of our employees applied to work with us specifically to learn the ropes of building for investment, and in return for his value to the company, we're helping him analyze and navigate his first deal. This illustrates how having the right guidance and support can ensure your first build is successful by helping you avoid costly mistakes.

There are several mistakes investors make during their first build, but by being aware of these common mistakes and their solutions, you'll have a much better chance of navigating your first project successfully:

NOT DOING SUFFICIENT RESEARCH BEFORE PURCHASING A LOT:

Thoroughly researching the lot and the surrounding market is crucial to avoid costly mistakes. Before making a purchase, consider factors like the market, zoning, and potential construction costs. Buying a lot without understanding these factors can lead to unforeseen issues eventually.

Solution:

Make your offer conditional upon financing and securing a building permit. You may want to include other conditions depending on the situation, but these two are critical. Conduct a thorough pre-consultation with the municipality and key professionals, including a designer, architect, and possibly soil experts. Avoid rushing into a deal until you are confident in your research. For a detailed guide, see Chapter 8: Analyzing a Potential Land Deal.

UNDERESTIMATING COSTS AND FINANCING:

Many people underestimate construction costs, assuming a build will be far cheaper than it actually is. Construction expenses vary widely based on the region, the lot, required permits, development charges (DCs), and finishes. Misjudging these can leave you in a financial bind, scrambling to secure additional funds halfway through the build.

Solution:

Include contingencies in your budget and research costs thoroughly. Have a solid understanding of expenses, such as environmental studies, severances, and DCs. Get a few quotes for large-ticket items in the early stages, consult professionals, and ensure you're financially prepared. This is especially important in projects like building multi-family homes, where unexpected costs can severely affect your cash flow.

POOR PLANNING:

Inadequate or inefficient design can lead to wasted space, higher maintenance costs, and decreased property value. When planning your build, it's essential to consider factors like future upkeep, market trends, and functionality. If you design without considering these, you may end up with a property that's harder to rent or sell.

Solution:

Plan realistically and thoroughly from the start. Focus on both functionality and market demand. For more guidance, see Chapter 9: The Planning Phase.

UNDERESTIMATING THE PERMIT AND BUILDING PROCESS:

The permitting process can be a complex and time-consuming challenge. Misjudging it or neglecting to follow proper procedures, such as securing the right documents or insurance for trades, can lead to delays and fines.

Additionally, unexpected responsibilities that fall between trades can quickly escalate costs if they aren't managed properly.

Solution:

Prepare yourself by researching the permit process, scheduling, and hiring professionals to ensure everything runs smoothly. For more details on managing these elements effectively, see Chapters 11, 12 and 15: The Construction Budget, The Permit Process, and The Art of Project Management.

MAKING UNCOORDINATED ALTERATIONS:

Making design changes during the construction phase without coordinating with all trades can lead to costly mistakes. For example, altering plans after contractors have started work may cause delays, alignment issues, or require costly fixes later in the build.

Solution:

Ensure that any changes to your plans are communicated clearly to all trades involved, and always replace outdated plans with updated ones. This minimizes the chance of errors and ensures everyone is on the same page. Avoid making multiple changes after plans have been sent out to trades.

POOR PROJECT MANAGEMENT:

Inadequate project management can result in missed deadlines, budget overruns, and poor communication. Effective project management involves keeping a close eye on timelines, maintaining accurate documentation, and ensuring that all contractors and tradespeople are working efficiently.

Solution:

Have a clear project timeline and hire a capable project manager. Effective communication and organization are key. For more on managing projects successfully, see Chapter 15: The Art of Project Management.

CHOOSING THE WRONG CONTRACTORS:

Hiring contractors solely on cost or without proper vetting can lead to subpar work or missed deadlines. This can derail your project and cost more in the long run if the work needs to be redone.

Solution:

Vet contractors thoroughly. Check references, verify licensing and insurance, and get a detailed estimate. Be wary of unusually low bids, and trust your instincts when selecting tradespeople. Aim to work with contractors who have a solid track record.

I'm not sharing these mistakes to scare you — I'm sharing them so you can step into this process with your eyes wide open. Building can be incredibly rewarding, but only if you're prepared. The truth is, even with guidance, you'll still hit bumps in the road. That's part of the journey.

The key is to minimize *avoidable* mistakes. Do your research. Ask questions. Don't rush. Get quotes. Vet your trades. Stay organized. And don't be afraid to lean on others who've done it before — whether that's a mentor, a contractor, or a company like ours.

You don't need to know everything — you just need to stay curious, be willing to learn, and surround yourself with the right people. That's how you'll turn your first build into a solid success story, and not just a survival tale.

TOP THREE TAKEAWAYS:

1. **Start Small and Be Flexible:** Getting into Build to Rent (BTR) doesn't require a massive, multi-unit project out of the gate. If financing isn't feasible for 4+ units, it's better to scale back than give up. Begin with a single-family home or duplex — and if needed, implement a "Training Wheels" strategy by designing the property with future conversion in mind. This flexibility allows you to pivot as needed while building experience and equity.

2. **Financing is the First Major Hurdle — But Not the End:** Getting financing, especially for your first project, is often the toughest part. Expect setbacks and be ready with a Plan B, whether it's leveraging a HELOC, downsizing your initial plan, or creatively structuring your project to make it more appealing to lenders. Each project adds credibility to your portfolio, which strengthens future financing options.

3. **Mistakes, Learning Curves, and the Power of a Long-Term Mindset:** Your first deal is about learning, not maximizing profit. You'll make mistakes, work long hours, and feel overwhelmed — but this education is essential. Avoid common pitfalls by doing thorough research, understanding true cash flow (not just rent minus mortgage), and having an exit strategy. With the right guidance and patience, your first build becomes the foundation for a scalable and sustainable investment strategy.

CHAPTER 5

GETTING FINANCED

Granting loans for new construction projects poses a greater risk for banks as they do not want to repossess a partially built home, which would be difficult to sell. Partially built homes often require additional capital to complete, can sit unsold for extended periods, and may not meet building codes—making them less appealing and more costly for banks to offload. This is one of the reasons why many banks reject loan applications for new builds, especially from first-time applicants with no construction background or solid financial history. The criteria for these loans can be rigorous, meaning they'll be looking for harsher minimum requirements when looking at the debt-to-income ratio, the credit history, the down payment, etc. And any income that is not straightforward or within the lender's typical "box" may not be accepted.

However, every lender is unique, with their own policies and procedures, and getting approved for a construction loan is not impossible. If one lender declined your application, would you consider that as an opportunity to re-evaluate why it was denied and try again with a different one? You may need to approach several lenders before getting approval, and you will require creativity and maybe the help of a knowledgeable broker who understands the process. Check with your lawyer, accountant or real estate agent for a referral to a good broker.

GENERAL RULES FOR CONSTRUCTION LOANS

Here are a few "general rules of thumb" to keep in mind before applying for loans at financial institutions:

- **Down payment:** A loan for just vacant land can require a down payment as high as 50 percent and will come with higher interest rates most of the time.

- **12 month commitment:** If you commit to starting the build within a year, you can sometimes lower the down payment requirement by buying an already serviced lot with the correct zoning. From what I remember when we purchased our first serviced lot in 2014 for our home, committing to building within the year reduced the down payment requirement to 0 percent. Meaning they fully funded the land and incorporated it into our construction loan. Keep in mind though that these were simpler times and for an-owner occupied home considered under residential lending, whereas today Rob and I are considered under commercial lending and the terms are more strict.

- **Using a HELOC:** If you have a second mortgage, such as a HELOC, it can be used to purchase land at a lower interest rate. This is how we typically purchase our lots in order to secure the deal quicker and until we work out the construction loans.

- **Construction Loan Features**: Typical construction loans can provide funding to include the land purchase. If the build is for five units or more, it's usually considered a commercial mortgage, which can mean that interest rates will be higher than, and the terms will differ from, a typical construction loan for four units or less.

- **Larger Developments**: Financing for larger projects often requires additional steps and becomes significantly more complex. But what actually counts as a "large" development? While there's no one-size-fits-all answer, most banks and lenders tend to categorize developments like this:

↳ **Small Development** – 1 to 4 units
These typically qualify for residential financing and are assessed using your personal income and debt servicing.

↳ **Medium Development** – 5 to 20 units
Once you hit 5 units, you're usually entering the world of commercial lending. You may still be eligible for better terms if you're working with an experienced broker or getting CMHC-insured financing (if applicable).

↳ **Large Development** – 20+ units or a total project budget of $5 million+
This is when lenders really start applying the pressure. You're dealing with layered financing, detailed pro formas, third-party cost consultants, potential performance bonds, and sometimes needing signed leases or pre-sales before they'll give the green light.

The bigger the build, the more they'll want to see feasibility studies, servicing plans, environmental reports, and confirmation that you're not biting off more than you can chew. Some feasibility studies alone can cost between $50,000–$100,000 or more, depending on the size and scope of the project.

Banks want to know that you're not just dreaming big but planning smart—and that you've done this (or something close to it) before. Experience counts here more than ever.

• **Life insurance:** I'm not sure if it's because we now have a large portfolio and it's based on a certain threshold reached or if it's a new policy across the board, but since 2024 it has now become a requirement for us to have life insurance as part of our construction loans. Which means they literally needed blood for the loan approval. They sent someone to our house to do bloodwork, urine tests, check our blood pressure and ask us questions about our health habits and family history. Maybe one day they will ask for a first born child too.

The terms for construction loans change often and can be particular to each situation. What was the process for us years ago may no longer apply today. Similarly, the process with our financial institution today may not be the same for you. This is why you'll need guidance from a good local broker.

HOUSE HACKING

House hacking is a strategy that can make loan approval a lot easier. Like I mentioned before, lenders are often hesitant to finance new construction due to the perceived risks—such as the possibility of the build not being completed or difficulties securing tenants. However, house hacking—where you live in the property while renting out part of it—offers lenders added reassurance that the home will be occupied and generating income. This strategy can take many forms: renting out rooms in a single-family home, creating a basement or second-floor unit, or living in one unit of a duplex, triplex, or fourplex while renting the others. This approach not only supports your loan application but also helps offset your own housing costs as you scale your rental portfolio.

This hack might be the best way to get started in BTR, and any other real estate investing strategy for that matter. It not only simplifies the loan approval process but also provides a history and experience for the borrower that builds trust with lenders and creates equity for future projects.

For example, when we had the plans of our 1,500-square-foot home appraised, it was appraised as a single-family home. After completing the basement apartment and renting it out, the lender revised and increased the home's value, allowing us to add a HELOC. Which, as we covered earlier, helped us finance the build for our first investment property. House hacking as a general strategy is perfect for getting into your first or next property.

It can also be a mindset shift—it's not always glamorous, and it may require some sacrifice in privacy or lifestyle at first. But it's one of the most effective ways to live for free or nearly free while building equity and credibility as a borrower. Many investors I know started this way and used it as a stepping stone to much larger portfolios. You don't need to commit to it forever—just long enough to get your foot in the door and establish yourself as someone who can manage tenants, maintain a property, and see a project through. That alone gives you a huge edge when applying for your next loan or presenting your next build to a private lender.

Let's dive into how we pulled off our first—and only—House Hack and built our very first home. We had a tenant in our home for 10 years while growing our business—but that was our personal choice. You don't have to commit that long. Still, once you get a taste of that extra cashflow, it's hard to let it go.

OUR FIRST CONSTRUCTION: BUILDING OUR HOME

Our journey into new construction began with building our own home, which we knew we had to house hack in order to afford it. This 1,500 sq/ft bungalow, constructed in 2014 when we were only 21 years old, has been our beloved home ever since. Using an Auto Construction loan – I'll explain what this is later – we completed the build impressively in less than four months. We broke ground by pouring the footings on July 22, 2014, and moved in on November 1st of the same year. House hacking for our first build has been one of our best decisions. Today, the basement apartment could easily rent for $1,700 or more—even with the poor soundproofing we installed back then, simply because we didn't yet know how to do it properly.

WHAT IS AN AUTO-CONSTRUCTION LOAN?

An Auto-Construction Loan, also called an owner-builder loan (or a construction-to-permanent loan in the U.S.), is a specialized loan for individuals managing their own construction projects. These loans are generally limited to personal homes or small investment properties.

They allow borrowers to use sweat equity—the value of their labor—in place of a cash down payment, reducing the upfront financial burden. Basically, we needed to get in there and pour some blood, sweat and tears, but we didn't need to put up a penny. However times have changed since our approval back in 2014 and the loan approval process isn't as simple as it once was.

When we applied then, we needed to submit architectural drawings, lot details (we only had an accepted offer on the land, we didn't own it yet), a construction budget, and other financial documents (papers like income tax statements, employment letters, etc).

They then had our house plans appraised by a professional appraiser who determined a value of let's say 100,000$ for easy math. The bank agreed to give us a loan for 80,000$, which is 80 percent of the value, and it was up to us to build it for that amount. No need to put a penny of our own money in it unless we went over budget, then it would have been our responsibility to pay the difference.

Once approved, they didn't just give us the entire 80k and said "Good luck!" Instead, funds were disbursed in stages based on construction progress, verified through site appraisals. When we needed an advance we would let the lender know, and they sent the appraiser on-site to do a progress report for them. The bank would send us the amount of money that corresponded based on their specific guidelines. Keep in mind, every time you call for an advance you have to pay the appraiser fees which are a few hundred dollars. Every dollar counts when you're trying to stay on budget, so you try to do as few as possible.

The final advance we got was at 100 percent completion, where they gave us the remainder of the budget, minus ten percent. In Ontario they hold back ten percent until 60 days after completion to make sure there are no liens* on the property. When the 60 days are up, this is where you get the last ten percent and you lock in your rate to convert the loan to a traditional mortgage.

TIP: A lien on a property is like a legal claim that a lender or creditor has on the property when it's used as collateral for a loan. If the borrower doesn't pay back the loan, the lender or creditor has the right to take possession of the property. In general, anyone who has a legal claim against a property can put a lien on it. That could include lenders, such as mortgage companies or banks, who have provided a loan to the property owner, or contractors who have performed work on the property but haven't been paid. Tax authorities can also place a lien on a property if the owner hasn't paid their property taxes.

HOW WE SAVED MONEY

To maximize our budget, here's what we did ourselves for this project:

- Project manager and general contractor
- The architectural drawings (the homeowner can do their own drawings in Ontario without needing an architectural stamp. Given our background we were able to do this)
- Framing of the basement perimeter walls
- Electrical (the homeowner can do their own electrical in Ontario as long as they get an Electrical Safety Authority permit)
- Drywall install and taping
- Trim work
- Flooring
- Cabinetry (thank you Ikea!)
- Paint and all other finishing

We also saved money by sourcing materials strategically:
- We got our tile on sale for 0.60$/sqft
- We got our hardwood flooring on sale for 3.49$/sqft
- Almost all of our plumbing fixtures we got free from a big renovation job my dad was doing. The client was gutting his not-so-old home and redoing everything so we took it! Free stuff!
- The stuff we couldn't get on sale we got basic models and upgraded later on
- We ripped MDF (Medium Density Fiberboard) to do all the baseboards and casings.
- Installing Ikea cabinets ourselves saved us a tone (we went with their low to moderate-priced styles)
- Appliances we either bought used on Kijiji (the canadian version of Craigslist) or at Home Depot using their promotional interest-free credit card

You can easily blow a budget way out of the water when shopping for the finishing items. This same house could have cost so much more if we would have gone for the expensive tile, fancy kitchen and exotic fixtures. We kept it simple and figured in the worst case we'll upgrade it later. I got to say though it looked pretty good for a kitchen that cost us only about 6,000$ in total (*including* appliances) This photo was taken back in . It looks pretty much the same today, although we eventually upgraded the fridge, stove, hoodfan, light fixtures and now have quartz countertops instead of standard laminate.

REBATES AND GRANTS

Shortly after completing our build, we applied for a government grant to recover some of the taxes we had paid. Both Canada and the U.S. offer various tax rebates, incentives, and exemptions for building new homes, though they vary by location and program. It's best to check local and state/provincial programs for specific rebates available in your area.

In Ontario, homebuyers typically don't pay sales tax on a newly purchased home. However, when you build a home, you do pay taxes on materials and labor during construction. To offset this, the government offers a rebate for a portion of these taxes. The process, however, can be complex. Especially for investment properties. Consulting a knowledgeable accountant or tax professional is crucial, because navigating these regulations is never straightforward.

In the case of our home, since we love DIYing so much, we tried to do the rebate program ourselves and received $12,000. Yet, apparently, we learned this a couple years later, we could have received up to 24k. Lesson learned: Pay for CPAs people!

Anyway, we used that money to jump-start the construction of the basement apartment, which we financed further using Home Depot's 18-month interest-free credit card for materials. At the time, we rented that 2-bedroom basement unit for 1,000$ a month. Imagine how excited we were. We were in our early twenties, living in a brand-new home we had built—and thanks to the rental income from our basement unit, our monthly housing costs were just a fraction of what they would've been otherwise.

AUTO-CONSTRUCTION LOANS VS. TRADITIONAL CONSTRUCTION LOANS

- **Auto-Construction Loans:** Designed for self-managed personal projects, such as building your own home. These loans often allow sweat equity to count toward the down payment and are typically suited for smaller-scale residential builds.

- **Traditional Construction Loans:** Usually require hiring licensed builders or contractors, as lenders often need to approve the builder's credentials and verify their licensing and insurance. These loans also emphasize adherence to detailed construction plans and timelines.

It's important to note that while traditional construction loans often require professional builders, some lenders may offer owner-builder loans to borrowers with construction experience. In our case, given our experience, the loans we secure today are essentially owner-builder commercial construction loans.

AUTO-CONSTRUCTION LOANS IN TODAY'S WORLD

The game has changed a bit since 2014 when it comes to auto-construction loans. Lenders are stricter now, and they're more cautious about self-managed construction projects. Sweat equity can still count as part of the down payment with some lenders, but you'll likely need to shop around and make a strong case for yourself. Expect them to want a solid financial position, a detailed project plan, and perhaps a couple more hoops to jump through.

For example, TD Canada Trust and RBC both have construction loan products, but whether or not they'll factor in sweat equity is usually a case-by-case decision. Having some construction experience under your belt can go a long way. Lenders want to see that you know what you're doing and can actually finish the project.

Like I've said before, having an experienced mortgage broker on your side is a must. Financing rules change all the time, and they can help you figure out which lenders are the best fit for your situation.

Start with a preconsultation with a bank to see what all the requirements would be, and then have everything ready to go before you officially apply for financing. Usually that means finalized construction plans, timelines, budgets, proof of your qualifications to take on the work and all your financial documents. I get that this can feel risky to design the house and everything without guaranteed financing, but showing lenders how prepared and serious you are can make the difference. However the preconsultation should have painted a clear picture of what the lender needs from you before starting the process.

I want to clarify that these loans are only available under personal banking, typically for projects like building your own home. If you're planning to build something larger, like an 8-unit property, that would automatically fall under commercial lending with a completely different process. In some cases, if your goal is to house-hack by living in one of the units, you might still qualify under personal banking, but you'd likely be limited to a fourplex at most.

TRADITIONAL CONSTRUCTION LOANS TODAY

Traditional construction loans aren't exactly a walk in the park these days, either. Most lenders now want a bigger cash down payment, even if you're acting as your own builder. That's their way of reducing risk. A lot of people end up combining personal savings or secondary financing to cover a chunk of the costs before the bank gives them the first draw. This is pretty much how we've been doing things.

And higher interest rates definitely aren't making things any easier. They mess with your debt-to-income ratio* and make it harder to qualify for the loan, so you'll need more cash reserves upfront. For example, when interest rates soared post pandemic, we worked with LTV ratios of 50 percent to 60 percent on most of our projects. That means the bank only funds 50 percent to 60 percent of the project's value, and we're responsible for the rest.

> TIP: Debt-to-income ratio (DTI) is a percentage that compares how much debt you owe to how much income you have. It's calculated by dividing your monthly debt payments (such as loans and credit card bills, for example) by your gross monthly income (how much money you make before taxes and other deductions). A lower DTI ratio means you have less debt relative to your income, which is generally seen as a good thing, while a higher DTI ratio means you have more debt relative to your income, which may make it harder to manage your payments and be viewed as a safe borrower.

I'd recommend checking out credit unions because they tend to be more flexible than traditional banks. If this is your first BTR project, shop around and talk to as many lenders as you can. Share your specific situation and show them what you bring to the table.

Once you've done a couple of projects, stick with the same lender if you can. Building a strong relationship with them can speed up the process when you're ready to scale. Relationships are everything in this business.

I'm not going to sugarcoat it—it's tough. But it's not impossible. You might just have to work a little harder for it. Don't throw in the towel yet though; there's always a way to make the numbers work. Keep reading.

UNDERSTANDING THE CONSTRUCTION LOAN PROCESS

Generally, the construction loan covers the cost of construction, including the land value. It's possible to arrange financing ahead of time in order to purchase the land with the loan. Personally, however, we've found that the financial approval process can be lengthy (I'm talking months sometimes), which makes it difficult to ask the seller to hold the land for you during that time. However, with the right circumstances—and a skilled negotiator—it can still be an option.

The loan amount is disbursed in stages as construction progresses. Interest payments are required during the building process, and you can draw on the loan amount within a set budget as construction progresses. Some lenders may require a downpayment and a deposit of funds before granting the first loan installment.

Here's a step-by-step look at how the process typically unfolds:

1. **Prequalification**: The borrower submits an application and supporting documentation to the bank, including financial statements, tax returns, and building plans. The bank evaluates the borrower's creditworthiness and ability to repay the loan.

2. **Loan Application**: If the borrower is pre-qualified, they complete a loan application and provide additional documentation, such as a construction budget and timeline, title report, and property appraisal.

3. **Loan under-writing**: The bank reviews the loan application and documentation to determine if the project meets its lending criteria. This includes evaluating the borrower's credit history, debt-to-income ratio, and the value and feasibility of the construction project.

4. **Loan approval**: If the bank approves the loan, it issues a commitment letter outlining the terms and conditions of the loan.

5. **Loan closing**: The borrower signs the loan documents, including the promissory note, mortgage, and other legal documents.

6. **Construction**: The bank then disburses the funds in stages as construction progresses. The borrower uses the loan funds to build the project, following the approved construction plan and timeline. Payments are made in interest-only form on the amounts drawn as construction progresses.

7. **Project Completion**: Once construction is complete, the borrower provides the bank with a final inspection report, occupancy permit, and other documentation as required. The bank may conduct its own inspection to verify that the project has been completed according to plan.

8. **Ten percent hold back**: In Ontario, the lender must retain ten percent of the remaining funds for 60 days after the project is 100 percent completed to ensure there are no liens on the property.

9. **Loan repayment**: The loan is then converted into a traditional mortgage and the borrower begins making payments.

Usually, the lender who provided your construction loan doesn't have to be the same one you work with for your mortgage after the construction is complete. However, verifying this beforehand and checking for any hidden fees or fine print is important. While you may prefer to continue working with the same lender as a sign of respect and to build a relationship, exploring other options is also acceptable. Don't become too fixated on getting approved with your preferred lender. Instead, focus on getting the construction loan first, and then you can shop for a mortgage toward the end of construction. But keep in mind that constantly switching lenders or inquiring with a large number of them and making them work for nothing can give you a bad reputation. Therefore, you should be discerning when shopping around.

To help you better understand what's required, I want to walk you through the exact process we follow today when securing financing for our construction projects.

When we first started, we bought and held properties under our personal names, so we followed personal banking rules. However, once you reach a certain threshold—like the bank's cap on the number of rental units you can own personally—they'll classify you as a business. This shift introduces new lending rules and criteria you'll need to adapt to. I'll dive deeper into opening corporations and different business structures in Chapter 17, but for now, here's a breakdown of the process we follow today under commercial banking:

1. **Appraisal**: We start by hiring an accredited appraiser to assess the architectural drawings. The appraiser will evaluate the property using the cost approach (construction cost), the income approach (property value based on income), and the comparison approach (value compared to similar properties).

This is typically how the market value is determined. Our lender usually provides a loan for somewhere up to 75 percent of the cost approach. See the next chapter to understand more about the Appraisal process.

2. **Loan qualification**: After we receive the appraisal report, we approach our lender to start the loan process. The lender will review our financial statements, property rent rolls, credit score, income, assets, and overall financial stability. We are also required to show that we have the required down payment available in some form, either in cash or from a line of credit. If you don't have it available, this is where you need to get creative. Consider involving a private lender (friends, family, or someone else you trust – as long as you put all the terms in writing).

3. **Loan disbursement**: Before the first loan disbursement, the construction must have progressed to the point where it reaches the value of the predetermined down payment.

Our goal is always to build for less than or equal to the amount the bank is lending us, **letting us recoup all our money from the down payment and recycle it into the next project.** If you've heard of the BRRRR strategy before, this is basically the same concept, except in this case, there's one less R. Instead of buy, renovate, rent, refinance, and repeat, our version is more like build, rent, refinance, and repeat.

BREAKING IT DOWN: SCENARIO BASED ON REAL NUMBERS

Below I'll provide an example of actual numbers and breakdowns from a triplex we built in 2024. It should help you understand how the loan and the draws were calculated with our chosen credit union. However, not all banks work the same. Honestly though, it might also confuse you. But I get asked this often, so I'm going to throw it in here, and hopefully it helps paint a picture in terms of the down payment you may need to front and for how long until you get all your money back.

Scenario from our Credit Union's Construction Loan process:

• Completed appraised Value: 985,000$

- Total construction costs (land + construction costs) = $975,545
  they took this number from the budget we sent them which is supported by the appraisal

- Land value = $178 000

- Direct construction costs = $797,545
  this is the total constructions costs minus the land value

- Holdback = ten percent
  this is how much they hold back for 60 days from the time you get Occupancy permit and the building is determined to be fully complete by the appraiser

- **Total loan amount = $685,000**
  This number was determined by the lender based on projected income, DTI, current rates and other internal factors and policies.

- Downpayment (Total construction costs – Loan amount) = $290,545

Now, on to the calculation. This credit union requires that we start the construction and get to a value equal to the required downpayment. Land value counts, so if you paid cash for the land, you have about 112k of valued work left to do before you can call for a draw. So, we paid the permit (in this case, the permit was cheaper at about 15k due to not having any DCs with an old house already existing on the property), then another 20k to demolish the old house. Now, getting the foundation in was about 30k, then the framing, another 35k. The roof, windows, and a couple other things. Let's say we've done all of that, so we call the appraiser to come inspect the progress to date. The appraiser determines that the project is at about 40 percent completion.

To start, let's figure out the progress report part:

- Progress report at 40 percent

- Construction costs according to 40 percent = $319,018 (Direct construction costs x 40 percent)

- Work progress + land = $ 497,018

Then:

- Work progress + land (minus) down payment = $206,473
- $206,473 (minus ten percent holdback) = $ 185,825.7
- $185,825.7 (minus) previous disbursements ($0 at this point) = $ 185,825.7

For future advances, you need to remember to deduct the previous disbursements. This means we are still about $311,192.3 in the red. (Work progress + land – this disbursement)

Now, let's say some time has passed and we are now progressing at about 65.5 percent.

- Construction costs according to 65.5 percent = $ 522,391.975 (Direct construction costs of 797,545 x 65.5 percent)
- Work progress + land = $ 700,391.98
- Minus down payment ($290,545) = $409,846.98
- $409,846.98 (minus ten percent holdback) = $ 368,862.28
- $ 368,862.28 minus previous disbursement of $ 185,825.7
- = $183,036.58

This means we are still about $331,529.7 in the red. (Work progress + land – both disbursements)

See a pattern? Feels like you'll never get there right? This is why it's important especially in the beginning of your investing journey if you don't already have capital to invest, to put in some sweat equity and save money. Alternatively, you could also rely on a private lender.

In the scenario described above, although the credit union's numbers and calculations are based on a true case from one of our builds, our actual direct construction costs, including the land, were closer to $630,000 (after the HST rebate and municipal performance deposits) instead of $797,545. I'd say approximately 40 percent of the build was done with our in-house team (Rob and Isaac, our general labour), the rest was outsourced to trades. Since the bank was offering a loan of $685,000, it means we still pulled out a profit of about 55,000$ from this build.

Not bad! But the numbers on our sixplexes are much more appealing. That's because the more rent you have under the same roof, the better it is. Fourplex numbers are usually good too.

To put this into perspective, given that the triplex was valued at $985,000, a $685,000 mortgage represents a 69.5 percent LTV ratio. This lower ratio reflects the impact of higher interest rates, which increase the overall debt-to-income ratio and limit the amount the bank is willing to lend. It's important to note that banks typically only loan *up* to 80 percent of the appraised value for new constructions.

That being said, we prefer smaller mortgages because they offer the best of both worlds: They keep us underleveraged while providing a large chunk of instant equity and significant monthly cash flow. As our portfolio, rental income, and financial stability grow, we feel more secure in our lifestyle.

Consequently, our goals are shifting. To achieve these new objectives, we are pivoting toward larger mortgages or joint ventures to cover costs of having more employees. While this strategy may offer less equity and cash flow, it helps with rapid growth and scaling operations.

FOR CANADIAN BUILDERS: CMHC-INSURED FINANCING (MLI SELECT)

If you're building a multi-unit property with 5 or more units, you've likely come across the CMHC MLI Select program—a government-backed mortgage insurance product offered through the Canada Mortgage and Housing Corporation. On paper, it offers major perks:

- Up to 95% loan-to-value (LTV)
- Amortizations up to 50 years
- Preferential interest rates
- Incentives for energy efficiency, affordability, and accessibility

It sounds like a dream for long-term buy-and-hold investors. But in reality? It's not for everyone.

Here's why:

- It's complex and bureaucratic. You often need to hire a CMHC-approved consultant just to navigate the paperwork and submit a qualifying application. Which can be expensive.

- There are strict eligibility requirements tied to your property's design, affordability of units, energy usage, and accessibility standards. Meeting these can add cost and design limitations.

- The timeline is long. CMHC approvals can take months and months—delaying your build or even your financing.

- And perhaps most concerning: at the end of your 5 year term, you're not guaranteed favorable terms or renewal at all for that matter. If your property doesn't continue to meet CMHC's ever changing criteria, you could end up stuck or needing to refinance elsewhere under less favorable terms.

- You also need to make sure your property is located within a CMHC-approved Census Metropolitan Area (CMA) or Census Agglomeration (CA) to even qualify. If you're building in a smaller town or rural area, you might be ineligible right from the start. This geographic limitation catches many builders off guard—so make sure your project falls within the designated areas before hiring a consultant or spending time applying.

Personally, I'd be more open to jumping through the hoops of the CMHC program if I were building something larger—like 9 units or more. But for our sixplexes, it just wasn't in the cards for us. The first didn't even qualify because it fell outside of the approved CMA area. For the second, we initially considered using our preferred lender during the build and then switching to CMHC for takeout financing—but the terms we got from our lender were so strong that the CMHC option just wasn't worth the hassle in the end. Plus, since we were doing the second one with a partner, we hadn't yet decided if we were ever going to sever the building in half, after which we would no longer qualify.

Explore the program with your eyes wide open, and talk to other investors who've gone through it. We have—and they all shared how discouraging the process was. That doesn't mean it wasn't worth it in the end. Like any tool, it's only as good as how you use it. Don't be afraid to say no if the program complicates more than it helps. But if it fits your project and timeline, it can be a powerful tool.

OTHER WAYS TO FINANCE A CONSTRUCTION

PRIVATE LENDING:

Private lending is generally more accessible than conventional lending because it involves less bureaucracy and fewer delays. However, it comes with higher interest rates and additional risks, such as the challenge of securing a traditional mortgage afterward. Typically, private lending also involves set-up fees and additional legal costs for both parties, but the interest rate is the biggest expense. For example, private lending rates might range from nine to 15 percent, compared to the prime + 1* rate from conventional construction loans from a bank.

> TIP: "Prime +1" refers to an interest rate that is one percentage point higher than the prime rate. The prime rate is the interest rate that commercial banks charge. It is often used as a benchmark for setting interest rates on various types of loans, including personal, business, and credit card loans.
>
> For example, if the prime rate is five percent, a loan or credit product with a "Prime +1" interest rate would have an interest rate of six percent. The "Prime +1" structure adjusts based on changes to the prime rate, so if the prime rate rises or falls, the "Prime +1" rate would adjust accordingly.

Private loans are still a great alternative though. They are usually intended for the duration of the construction project and can be included in the construction budget. To ensure full repayment to your lender, you must qualify for a mortgage upon completion of the build. In one instance, we borrowed privately for a fourplex and requested the loan in progressive cash advances, similar to a construction loan, allowing the interest to be paid in stages. Once construction was completed, we secured a conventional mortgage and fully repaid our private lender.

SELLER FINANCING:

We haven't done this strategy yet, but we have friends who have and the types of deals that came from it. This is where both parties can get creative as to how they want to form the arrangement. Essentially, seller financing is a strategy where the seller acts as the lender to the buyer, and the buyer makes regular payments with interest to the seller until the loan is paid off. In the case of Building-to-Rent, this would apply to buying the property you plan to build on, whether this is vacant land or a property with a house already on it that you plan to demolish and build something new. This strategy eliminates the need for third-party approval from banks or other lenders.

PARTNERSHIPS AND JOINT VENTURES:

One effective strategy for BTR is forming partnerships or joint ventures with high-net-worth individuals or investors who are interested in this strategy. These investors can provide the necessary capital and bring valuable experience to the table, making them ideal partners in your ventures. Seek guidance from your lawyer, accountant, or realtor, as they can often refer you to individuals who provide these types of services if you don't already have anyone in your network.

This underscores the importance of networking and building relationships in real estate. Attending real estate conferences, seminars, and industry events can help you connect with potential investors, lenders, and partners. Building a robust network can provide you with access to capital and valuable industry insights. Additionally, leverage online platforms, such as LinkedIn or real estate forums, to expand your reach and connect with like-minded professionals. Collaborating with other experienced investors allows you to pool resources, share expertise, and increase your access to potential capital sources, enhancing your BTR projects. Partnerships can also be formed with friends and family, though it's essential to proceed cautiously to avoid straining personal relationships.

Just note that there are a few key differences between a partnership and a joint venture. We are currently doing a Joint Venture with someone, and we chose this type of agreement based on a conversation between our accountant (who has done BTR projects himself with JVs before) and also with our lawyer who supported this type of agreement based on our specific situation. Discuss both types with these important key players in your team, and understand the differences before moving forward on one.

OTHER QUICK TIPS:

While we focus on more traditional methods in this book, there are a few other ways to help get your BTR project financed. Here's a quick list, but you'll need to do your own research:

- **Refinancing**: Refinance existing properties to access equity and reinvest in new projects. Just make sure not to overleverage your overall portfolio to manage risk.

- **Equity Partners**: Seek silent partners willing to invest capital into your projects, in exchange for equity.

- **Grants and Incentives**: Research local, state, or federal programs that provide funding for specific types of developments (e.g., affordable housing or green building).

- **Tax Credits**: Leverage tax credit programs, like Low-Income Housing Tax Credits (LIHTCs) or renewable energy credits, to attract investors.

- **Syndication**: Pool funds from multiple investors to finance larger projects, offering them shares in the deal. Make sure to research compliance and security laws.

- **Crowdfunding:** Online crowdfunding platforms can help to raise funds from multiple investors online. Make sure to research compliance and security laws.

COMBINING STRATEGIES:

Combining methods can be really advantageous. For example, you could combine traditional financing with seller financing if the bank doesn't provide enough funding. In such cases, the buyer can ask the seller to finance the remaining balance. The key to making this arrangement successful is finding a mutually beneficial solution, which can be challenging as sellers may prefer to receive the total purchase price upfront. Creativity and flexible deal structuring are necessary to make both parties happy.

You could also combine traditional financing with private lending for the down payment if you lack the capital to show the bank you have the necessary funds to get the project started while you wait for the first draw. You can even add a Joint Venture agreement in the mix of this last combo. Get creative!

TO SUMMARIZE:

Whichever way you choose to secure financing for your BTR project, it's essential to take these five steps for your method of choice to work, and for doors to start opening for you:

1. Build a solid track record: Demonstrating a successful track record is crucial in attracting investors. Highlight your past real estate deals, showcase their profitability, and provide references or testimonials from previous partners or clients.

2. Develop a detailed business plan: Create a comprehensive business plan that outlines your investment strategy, target market, financial projections, and risk mitigation strategies. This will instill confidence in potential investors and show that you have thoroughly considered the opportunities and challenges of your investments.

3. Personal savings: Investing your own money demonstrates your commitment to the venture and can attract other investors.

4. Create a compelling investor pitch: Craft a persuasive and well-prepared investor presentation that highlights the potential returns, market analysis, project details, and exit strategies.

5. Keep it legal and have contracts in place: Consult with legal and financial professionals to ensure compliance with securities laws and regulations when soliciting investments. It's crucial to adhere to the legal requirements of your jurisdiction to avoid any legal repercussions. Remember, building trust and

credibility as a real estate investor is essential when attracting potential investors and lenders. Providing transparent and accurate information, maintaining strong communication with investors, and delivering on your promises will help you establish a solid reputation and attract future investments.

POST-CONSTRUCTION FINANCING

Honestly in my experience, getting the loan to build is typically more challenging than acquiring the loan after it's built. The risk lies in the construction itself. If you can figure out a way to get short-term financing for the build part and get the signed leases, as long as the rent more than covers the expenses including the mortgage payment, you should have fewer problems getting the final mortgage. Lenders will closely examine your financial stability and creditworthiness as well. Even if you apply under a corporation or LLC, the owners of those are still financially liable and will be verified. This includes your credit score, debt-to-income ratio, and overall financial health.

Evidently, the lenders will also assess the completed property's value and its income potential. A property with high rental income potential and low vacancy rates is more attractive to lenders.

An appraisal will be conducted to determine the property's market value. Lenders typically have specific requirements for the LTV ratio. Having a higher amount of equity in the property can improve your chances of obtaining a loan and may result in better interest rates and terms. This is why focusing on a low construction cost is vital.

You'll need to include the following documentation:

- **Proof of income:** Tax returns, pay stubs, and financial statements.

- **Construction completion documents:** Proof that the construction is complete and meets all building codes and regulations, like the Occupancy report from your final inspection and a zoning certificate.

- **Lease agreements:** Copies of signed lease agreements.

- **Operating history:** If the property has been generating rental income for some time, detailed records of this income will be required.

If you're going with a private lender for the build, and you're nervous about qualifying for the long-term mortgage post-build, I'd recommend a consultation with a lender or broker before starting the build. Clearly articulate the purpose of the loan, bring all your financial documents including the budget, the appraisal (if required to be provided by you, I'll explain in the next section), your business plan and the anticipated rents. If you're unsure of how much the property will rent, check with a realtor or local property management company to see if they could print out a few comparable for you. Having a chat with a knowledge advisor pre-build can provide valuable guidance and set you up for success.

BREAKING IT DOWN: SCENARIO BASED ON REAL NUMBERS

It's always wise to plan for worst-case scenario rents and interest rates. Taking the earlier triplex example, we initially projected a total monthly income of $6,200 and a six percent interest rate. However, I was able to secure $6,475 a month with a 5.70 percent interest rate, resulting in an estimated monthly cash flow of approximately $1,200 after covering all expenses, including "ghost expenses" like vacancy and capital expenditures.

While you might consider suggesting higher rents to your appraiser at the project's outset to secure a larger loan, I'd advise against that. If market conditions shift during construction or if you find yourself overconfident after marketing the rental for several weeks without traction, you could face significant setbacks. Your loan amount may decrease, necessitating adjustments from your appraiser, which can leave you in a precarious position. It's always better to err on the side of caution.

TOP THREE TAKEAWAYS:

1. **Construction Loan Challenges and Solutions:** Securing loans for new construction projects is difficult due to the higher risk for lenders, especially for first-time applicants with no construction experience or solid financial history. The criteria for approval are strict, and unconventional income sources may not be accepted. However, persistence and creativity can help; if one lender rejects your application, consider re-evaluating the reasons for denial and applying to other lenders, potentially with the help of a knowledgeable broker.

2. **House Hacking as a Viable Strategy**: House hacking, or renting out part of your primary residence, simplifies the loan approval process and builds trust with lenders. This strategy provides a history of successful property management and creates equity for future projects, as demonstrated by our experience with our first home.

3. **There's always a way**: There's always a way to finance your BTR project if you remain flexible, creative, and resourceful. With options like private lending, seller financing, joint ventures, and alternative strategies such as refinancing or combining methods, the key lies in building strong relationships, planning carefully, and thinking outside the box. By leveraging the right combination of tools and strategies, even the most challenging financing scenarios can lead to success.

CHAPTER 6

THE APPRAISAL

The Appraisal is a crucial part of the entire Build & Hold process. It paints a very clear picture of your project before you start building and helps you determine whether the project will make sense, or if you need to make any adjustments. However, some banks prefer to order their own in-house appraisal, and may not share the report with the borrower.

> TIP: Before you go out to get an appraisal, I'd recommend discussing this with your preferred lender before to see what their protocol and policies typically are. Can you order your own report? If they need to order one in-house, will they share the report with you?

From personal experience, early on, our credit union handled the appraisal orders and didn't share the details with us, which was frustrating. This lack of transparency made it difficult for us to move forward with confidence. It wasn't until we switched from personal to commercial banking that we gained control over this process and were able to directly access the appraisal reports.

Based on that experience, I strongly recommend advocating for access to the appraisal report. Explain to your lender why understanding the numbers is crucial for the success of your project. If they still refuse due to their policies, but you're committed to working with them, you may allow them to proceed with ordering the appraisal—just be aware that you'll likely need to cover the appraisal fee.

Once you receive the final pre-approval loan amount, assess whether it aligns with your budget and cash flow projections. If the numbers make sense, you can choose to move forward. However, if they don't add up, I suggest hiring a private appraiser for your own assessment. This way, you'll have access to the report, allowing you to determine your next steps—whether that means redesigning the project, switching lenders, or even exploring alternative financing methods.

When ordering an appraisal, you'll need to provide the following:

1. The Address / Location

2. The Architectural Drawings

3. The Budget (sometimes they may also request to support this with actual estimates from trades)

4. The Anticipated Rents

5. The Specs (type of heating, finishes, etc.)

I'll start by explaining the appraisal process so you understand how an appraiser will value your project. Then I'll share numbers with you from a real-life example of one of our fourplex builds.

UNDERSTANDING THE APPRAISAL PROCESS

When appraising a new build, an appraiser evaluates its market value through three main approaches: The Cost Approach, the Sales Comparison Approach, and the Income Approach. Each method provides a unique perspective on the property's value and is selected based on the type of property and the appraisal's purpose.

1. COST APPROACH

The Cost Approach estimates the value of a property by calculating how much it would cost anyone to replace or reproduce it, minus depreciation. This is usually turn-key costs as if a general contractor was hired.

Process in a New Build Appraisal:

1. Estimate land value as if it were vacant.

2.   Calculate construction costs (turn-key costs as if fully built by a GC).

3.   Add land value to the total construction cost to determine the appraised value.

2. SALES COMPARISON APPROACH

The Sales Comparison Approach determines property value by comparing it to similar properties that have recently sold in the same area.

Process:

1.   Identify comparable properties that have sold recently.

2.   Adjust sale prices for differences in attributes.

3.   Use these adjusted prices to estimate the subject property's value.

3. INCOME APPROACH

The Income Approach estimates property value based on its potential to generate income, primarily used for income-producing properties.

Process:

1.   Estimate the Potential Gross Income (PGI): Total income if fully rented at market rates.

2.   Calculate the Effective Gross Income (EGI): Subtract expected vacancy and collection losses.

3.   Calculate the Net Operating Income (NOI): EGI minus operating expenses (excluding financing costs)

4.   Apply a Capitalization Rate (Cap Rate) to determine the property's value.

Appraisers often use a combination of these methods to determine a property's market value, weighing each approach based on its relevance to the property and the context of the appraisal. This provides a comprehensive and balanced value estimate.

PRACTICAL EXAMPLE

Let's say you want to build a fourplex and get it appraised first. The appraiser uses the three approaches and will assign a certain percentage of weight on each approach:

Cost Approach: $690,000 (20 percent weight)

Sales Comparison Approach: $750,000 (40 percent weight)

Income Approach: $790,000 (40 percent weight)

> To calculate the final value:
> Final Value=(690,000×0.20)+(750,000×0.40)+(790,000×0.40)
> Breaking it down:
> 690,000 × 0.20 = 138,000
>
> 750,000 × 0.40 = 300,000
>
> 790,000 × 0.40 = 316,000
> Adding these together:
> Final Value = 138,000 + 300,000 + 316,000 = 754,000
>
> The final appraised value of the fourplex would be $754,000.

REAL-LIFE EXAMPLE

Below are the results of an appraisal for a fourplex (a side-by-side duplex with basement units in each) we built in 2021. Now, I don't know the appraiser's exact calculations and weighted percentages, but it should show you how an appraisal paints a clear picture.

Sales Comparison Approach: $1,050,000 (525,000$ per side based on recent sales of similar homes)

Income Approach: $1,078,000 (based on potential rental income)
Effect Gross Income: 75,600$ - two percent vacancy = 74,088$
Operating Expenses: 20,204$ (taxes @ 9,600$, insurance @ 4,500$, repairs & maintenance @ 1,200$, PM @ 3,704$, snow & lawn @ 1,200$)
Net Income: 53,884$
Cap rate: Five percent
= Final value of 1,077,680$ rounded at 1,078,000$

In the Notes it is written as: *"The applicant indicates that the property will be tenant occupied. The main floor units will be offered at $1,700 and the basement units at $1,450 per month. The tenants are responsible for electricity, gas, water charges and phone/internet/cable charges. Vacancy rates in the area are currently low. Landlords indicate that there are very few vacancies and when a unit is vacant, they are easily re-rented. A vacancy rate of two percent is supported. A capitalization rate of five percent was well supported by comparable sales for newer modern small plex type buildings."*

Cost Approach: $881,400 (reflecting land value and how much it should cost to build*).

Floor area above grade: 2,200 square feet @ 225$ = 495,000$
Basement finished units: 2,200 square feet @ 100$ = 220,000$
Attached single car garages: 528 square feet @ 50 = 26,400$
Parking, Walkway, Porches + Site Improvements = 60,000$
Land cost: 80,000$

Notes: *"MINIMAL WEIGHT PLACED ON COST APPROACH."*
*It's important that the budget you provide is based on actual turn key costs, meaning what the market value of hiring for each trade would be, versus what your actual costs are. For example, if you were to hire a company to install the drywall versus if you install the drywall yourself, resulting in significant savings.

Final notes in the appraisal:

"The final estimate of market value is $1,065,000 AS THOUGH COMPLETE." (Direct Comparison Approach $1,050,000, Income Approach $1,078,000). This is based on a typical market exposure of up to 90 days. Most weight is placed on the Direct Comparison Approach and Income Approach with minimal weight placed on the Cost Approach."

The final Market Value was **1,065,000$**

Seeing as the anticipated rent amounts were conservative, and that the numbers worked for us with our actual costs being estimated at about 656,000$, we were comfortable moving forward with the build.

We ended up renting the top units for 1,900$ + utilities, and the basement units for 1,600$ + utilities. The credit union we typically work with offered us a loan for 698,000$. This is about 80 percent of the Cost Approach, or 65 percent LTV. You're probably thinking that's too low, but this number covered all our costs and some, keeping us underleveraged with a positive cash flow of 1,200$ a month even with a three year fixed rate of 6.03 percent. Keep in mind, we could have asked the bank to revise and increase the loan seeing as the income ended up being higher than anticipated. But we were good with those numbers.

Appraisers use professional judgment to weigh the values from each approach rather than averaging them. This ensures the final market value reflects the most reliable and relevant data for the property. The reconciliation process integrates all available information, providing a comprehensive and accurate market value estimate.

TAKING THE 'BRRRR' METHOD TO A NEW LEVEL

I touched a little bit about this earlier, but I want to dive in further now. If you haven't heard of the BRRRR method before, it stands for **Buy, Renovate, Rent, Refinance,** and **Repeat**. This strategy is a powerful way for investors to build a portfolio of rental properties while minimizing the need for large, upfront capital. Essentially, it allows you to continually recycle your capital, meaning you can keep using the same initial investment to acquire more properties over time. Let's break down each step in more detail.

Buy: The first step is to purchase a distressed property at a below-market price. Typically, this property will need significant repairs or renovations—hence the term "distressed." The goal here is to buy low, with the understanding that you'll add value through the renovation process. These properties are often overlooked by traditional buyers due to their condition, but they offer a great opportunity for investors who are willing to put in the work.

Renovate: After purchasing the property, the next step is to renovate it to increase its value. The improvements made during this stage could range from cosmetic updates, like painting and flooring, to more significant renovations, such as kitchen or bathroom upgrades, roofing, or addressing structural issues. The key here is to focus on cost-effective upgrades that will maximize the return on investment. The goal is to raise the property's value enough to justify a higher appraisal for refinancing. It's important to keep track of renovation costs and timelines, as delays or cost overruns can eat into potential profits.

Rent: Once renovations are complete, the next step is to rent the property. Renting it out ensures you have a steady income stream, which can be used to pay down the mortgage and cover operating expenses.

Refinance: After the property is rented, you can refinance it based on its new, higher market value post-renovation. This is where the magic of the BRRRR method really happens. A refinance allows you to pull out some of the equity you've built through the renovation. Ideally, this process will allow you to recoup most, if not all, of your initial investment. By refinancing, you secure a new mortgage that is based on the appraised value of the property after renovations. This new loan often has a lower interest rate than the initial purchase loan, which helps to maximize your cash flow going forward.

Repeat: The final step is to repeat the process. With the cash pulled from the refinance, you can go back to the market and buy another distressed property to renovate, rent, and refinance again. The more you repeat the cycle, the faster your portfolio can grow, without needing to continually invest large amounts of new capital. Essentially, you're using the appreciation from each property to fund future acquisitions, scaling your real estate portfolio over time.

OUR APPROACH: THE BRRR

This is basically the same process we use, except our version includes one less R in the title. **BRRR: Build, Rent, Refinance,** and **Repeat.** By starting with a blank canvas rather than renovating an existing structure, we gain even greater control over the design, functionality, and cost effectiveness of the property.

Take the real-life example from before: By getting a loan of $698,000 when the construction cost us a total of $656,000, we recycled every single penny we initially invested and we pulled out $42,000 at the end. Here's how it worked:

- **Land purchase**: $78,000
- **Build cost**: $578,000
- **Total cost**: $656,000
- **Refinanced mortgage**: $698,000
- **Total money invested**: $0
- **Profit**: $42,000
- **Monthly cash flow**: $1,200

Imagine that you purchase the land using a line of credit (LOC). You then utilize more of your LOC to start the build process until you earn your first draw from the construction loan. You can then continue with the higher-interest, short-term construction loan until the build is complete. At that point, you refinance with a long-term, traditional mortgage, that allows you to pay back the construction loan *and* reimburse your LOCs in full, plus have an extra 42k.

If you weren't hooked on building to rent before, I bet you are now!

Our version of BRRR offers immense scalability for investors looking to grow their portfolios. You can create a self-sustaining cycle that funds itself by reinvesting the proceeds from refinances into subsequent projects. Over time, this strategy not only builds wealth but also provides a steady cash flow to support future endeavors.

It's also worth noting the broader impact of this strategy. BTR contributes to community development by increasing the availability of quality housing. You can align your investment goals with positive societal outcomes by focusing on well-designed, energy-efficient and more affordable properties.

With the right approach, this method can transform your financial future while contributing to the development of better communities.

TOP THREE TAKEAWAYS:

1. **Understanding Appraisals for the BTR process**: The appraisal is essential in the Build & Hold process as it provides a detailed picture of a project's financial viability before construction begins. Discussing the appraisal process with your lender is crucial because some banks may prefer in-house appraisals and might not share the report with the borrower. Understanding their protocols and policies can help you determine if you can order your own appraisal or if you need to rely on the lender's appraisal.

2. **Different Approaches to Appraisals**: Appraisers use three main methods to evaluate the market value of new builds:

   • **Cost Approach**: Estimates the value based on the cost to replace or reproduce the property in the absence of depreciation. It includes factors like land value, replacement cost, reproduction cost, and depreciation.

   • **Sales Comparison Approach**: Determines value by comparing the property to similar properties that have recently sold in the same area. It adjusts for differences between comparable properties and the subject property.

   • **Income Approach**: Estimates value based on the property's potential to generate income. It calculates potential gross income, effective gross income, net operating income, and applies a capitalization rate to determine market value.

3. **Real-Life Example using the BRRR method**: We used a real-life example from a fourplex built in 2021 to demonstrate how the appraiser used the three methods to determine the final value of the property at $1,065,000, primarily based on the Sales Comparison and Income Approaches. This example then highlights the utilization of the BRRR method to recycle capital and continue growing your portfolio rental properties.

CHAPTER 7

FINDING LAND DEALS

Finding the right piece of land is one of the most important steps in any new construction project. But not all land is created equal. Some lots are fully serviced and ready to build on, while others require a ton of work (and money) just to get them to that point. The difference between the two can massively impact your timeline, budget, and overall project success.

In this chapter, I'll break down the key differences between raw and serviced lots, sharing our own experience with both—including a multi-year battle to develop a raw land parcel that we thought would take half the time. I'll also walk you through different ways to actually find land deals, from MLS to networking to leveraging expired listings. Whether you're just getting started or looking to scale, understanding how to evaluate and secure the right lots will set you up for success.

DIFFERENTIATING RAW LAND VS. SERVICED LOTS

In real estate development, **raw land** refers to land that has not been improved with essential infrastructure like water, sewage, electricity, or roads. While it offers the potential for development, it requires significant work to make it buildable. On the other hand, **serviced lots** come with these utilities and services already in place, making them ready for immediate construction.

The allure of raw land often presents itself as an exciting opportunity—a blank canvas brimming with potential, especially when the purchase price is on the lower end. However, developing raw land comes with challenges, expenses, and time-consuming processes that can overwhelm even seasoned developers. This is why we typically prefer to purchase serviced lots that are ready for construction, as it mitigates many risks such as not being granted proper approvals and having to hold all the costs for several years. It simplifies the journey from acquisition to project completion.

Back in 2020, we acquired a 2.8-acre parcel of raw land zoned for commercial use, intending to transform it into a multi-phase residential project. We knew it would take time—initially anticipating a couple of years—but it ended up taking four years from purchase to permits. During this time, we had to shrink Phase 1 just to see any progress.

The first hurdle was a hydrogeological assessment and terrain analysis to determine if the land could support private septic systems since municipal sewers were unavailable. We also navigated the bureaucratic process of public hearings and zoning changes from commercial to residential. These steps, combined with the regulatory approvals, were lengthy.

During the four years it took to move this project forward, we completed five other projects on serviced lots. This just goes to show how challenging it can be to deal with improperly zoned land and extensive regulatory requirements. (Also quick side note: If you're wanting to finance a piece of land that doesn't have the proper zoning for your intended build purpose, it will often negate financing. Like in our case, since the land was zoned commercial but our goal was to build a residential project, it made financing more challenging. Lenders are usually wary of the added risk in case the zoning change application gets refused.)

Since the entire process was taking so long, we faced the critical decisions of changing the scope of Phase 1. Initially, we planned to build a nine-unit building, but as delays mounted, we opted to reduce this to a six-unit structure. Without going into all the technical jargon and local by-laws, we basically did this because it allowed us to pass the project under smaller residential processes and speed up the permit process, not to mention cut the development fees to a fraction thanks to Ontario's new Bill 23. (More about this in Chapter 10)

Another significant decision we faced was changing our civil engineering firm in the final year of the planning process. After three and a half years of slow progress and mounting frustration, we realized that this initial firm was not proactive enough. Switching firms was a difficult decision, because we don't like to burn bridges nor pay for the same services twice, but it was essential for accelerating the project. Sometimes you have no choice but to shift gears. In the end, we were mad at ourselves for not switching sooner. The new firm delivered lightning fast and at a much cheaper price.

Had we bought serviced land, the purchase price would have been higher—about 1.5 times more. However, by purchasing raw land at $210k, we added significant value through zoning changes and studies, eventually increasing its value to somewhere between $375-$450k. Granted, some of that might be attributed to inflation over the years we held it, but the time and effort we invested also increased its worth exponentially.

Despite the lengthy process, this project should be one of our best deals once all phases are complete. If we ever get there. Developing the land ourselves allowed us to customize services and maximize the number of units, ultimately making the numbers work in our favor.

I think a balanced approach can be interesting. If you have the resources and capital, you could invest in several ready-serviced lots that are quick and easier to monetize, alongside a raw land opportunity similar to ours. You could develop and monetize the ready-serviced lots while working on the more complex raw ones. This strategy ensures a steady flow of projects, but I definitely do not recommend this for those starting out in the new construction game. It can be very risky to hold and manage several types of projects at once.

Even if you're an experienced investor but you're new to new construction, I recommend starting slow on your first couple builds. Buy and Hold is not the same game as Build and Hold. Start with a serviced lot. One of the most compelling reasons is the reduced time to build. With a serviced lot, you can start construction much sooner. After securing your architectural plans, grading plans, financing, and a few other details, you're often shovel-ready, significantly shortening the project timeline.

Moreover, serviced lots offer more predictable costs, making budgeting easier. With raw land, unexpected expenses, such as soil remediation or regulatory compliance, can quickly escalate. You may also need to install infrastructure like water, sewage, electricity, and roads—expenses that serviced lots already account for, eliminating these upfront investments.

My lawyer once told us: "There are two things that can tank a business. Lack of income, and scaling too quickly". That always stuck with me. It kept me from taking on large complex projects like those and kept me grounded.

WAYS TO FIND LAND DEALS

MULTIPLE LISTING SERVICE (MLS)

The Multiple Listing Service (MLS) is a centralized database where real estate professionals list properties for sale, making it one of the most widely used tools for buyers and investors. While some real estate gurus might claim that finding great deals on MLS is a thing of the past, I strongly disagree. In fact, 75 percent of our lot purchases were found through MLS, and many of them were fantastic deals!

I admit that during Covid high-market times, it was almost impossible to find great deals through MLS. But when times are normal it's always possible. Truth is, I'm too lazy to navigate all the other methods for finding off market deals. I could put my virtual assistant on top of that, but back when I didn't have a VA, I did not take the time to do anything fancy other than search on MLS. If MLS and word-of-mouth are still working for me, I don't see why it wouldn't work for you either.

I recommend working with a realtor who not only knows the market but also has a good understanding of construction and investing. They can provide valuable guidance and help you find listings that are appropriate for you. As a licensed realtor, I closely monitor the MLS database and the local market. I recommend that you be added to your realtor's email notification system, which will inform you of new lot listings and conditional sales in the area you're investing in, and keep you informed of the latest market activity.

You can also create your own notification email through listing websites. Take Realtor.ca (or .com) for instance, once you download the app and create an account, under the search bar, click on filters, type in the city you're searching for as a location, select "Vacant Land" as the property type, add a price range if you wish, then hit Results. Once the list appears, hit the Save button on the left-hand side of the search bar, give a name to your search and save that. Now, every single "vacant land" listing that will go on the market in your selected city will send you a notification on the App and an email. You could create several searches like this to include properties that also have homes on them with the potential to tear down and rebuild.

The notification system should only be a back up as you should still consider working with an agent. Before I became a real estate agent, we valued having a solid working relationship with a realtor who always looked out for our interests. Even though realtors have ethical obligations, we were always a little worried that the listing agent would prioritize the seller's needs over the buyer's. Therefore, we preferred to have an agent working on our behalf to obtain information instead of contacting the listing agent directly. The benefit of this was a more objective negotiation process, free of emotional attachment, that secured the best deals for us.

Yet on the other hand, working with only the listing agent might help secure a better deal if the agent is willing to reduce their commission seeing as they don't need to share it with another agent.

EXPIRED LISTINGS

Working with a realtor can also give you access to expired listings–properties that were listed for sale but did not sell before their listing expired. Your realtor can give you a list of these properties to review. You can then request your realtor to contact the relevant agents and ask about the reasons for the lack of a sale and whether the seller is still interested.

While this method can be time-consuming and may not always lead to a successful deal, it is still worth considering. It just takes one good deal to pay back that time and make it all worth it. Does it ultimately result in getting a cheaper deal? Especially as the listing didn't get the desired outcome at first? Maybe, maybe not. I mean it definitely could, but there's only one way to know for sure. Try it, then let me know!

Just keep in mind that this process can consume a significant amount of your realtor's time, so don't let it go unnoticed, and offer something in return.

NETWORKING, RELATIONSHIPS AND WORD OF MOUTH

Networking and word of mouth are powerful tools for uncovering land deals. Building and leveraging connections can open doors to opportunities that may have otherwise remained hidden. One of the best ways to start is by joining local real estate investment groups or clubs. These groups are filled with other investors and landowners who can share valuable insights and opportunities. Networking within these groups allows you to learn from others' experiences, get advice, and potentially find partners for future projects. You can also attend real estate conferences, seminars, and local community events. They're usually prime opportunities to connect with potential sellers, learn about market trends, and make valuable contacts. Being active in the real estate community not only increases your visibility but also your credibility.

Leverage your network of real estate professionals, including lawyers, contractors, and architects. These individuals often have insider knowledge about land deals and can provide referrals. They might be aware of properties before they hit the market or know of landowners looking to sell. A casual conversation with our lawyer or accountant occasionally led to whispers of a new opportunity. We quickly learned that these professional relationships were goldmines of information and potential deals. Our lawyer directly sold us his property once so we could build a fourplex, and another time he even lent us money for another project.

Social media has also been a game-changer for us in attracting deals. Simply making it known that we were in the market for land would bring several opportunities. We actively shared our projects on social media platforms like Facebook and Instagram, making it easy for others to reach out and discuss potential. Sharing progress on multiple builds proved especially effective. By doing this, we generated buzz not only among our friends and family but also within a wider audience. People became curious about our work, leading to inquiries and offers. Using social media platforms like Facebook and LinkedIn to run ads targeting landowners in your desired locations can be highly effective. Additionally, posting your buying criteria on platforms like Craigslist and Facebook Marketplace can attract potential sellers.

Once, someone approached us about a piece of land he owned right in front of one of our builds. He liked what we were doing and ended up selling us part of his property. This opportunity arose simply because we were visible and actively sharing our progress online. Another effective strategy is putting up signs with your website around town or during a build. This can catch the attention of passersby and direct them to your website showing your projects. Sharing your plans with friends and family and asking them to spread the word can also be helpful.

Although it may be nerve-wracking to be open about your plans, especially if you're anxious about what people will think, you never know when a random conversation will lead to valuable leads or market insights. Sometimes, you need to put yourself out there. Just be mindful not to overdo it and become "that person who never shuts up about real estate." Balancing visibility and approachability is the key.

REACH OUT TO PRIVATE SELLERS

Platforms like Facebook and LinkedIn can allow you to run targeted ads in specific areas, and hopefully that will entice a few landowners to call you. Posting your buying criteria on Kijiji (or Craigslist) and Facebook Marketplace can yield surprising results too. These online marketplaces can connect you with landowners who are looking to sell but haven't listed their properties publicly yet. Any call has the potential to become an interesting discussion, and become either a strategic connection or hopefully a good deal.

Another approach that has worked well for us is connecting with landlords advertising units for rent or sale on these platforms. In our case, however, it was a landlord who reached out to me when I was advertising a unit for rent because they wanted to sell an older property. We visited it since it had redevelopment potential but ultimately passed it on to a friend who purchased it instead. Many landlords own more than just the one property they're advertising. Some may be looking to offload a few, have older properties ripe for infill projects, or even own excess land that could be severed. They might also be interested in partnering with someone more experienced—like you! A simple, friendly message to someone on Facebook can lead to a much bigger conversation. Like-minded investors often love chatting about real estate, and these discussions can open doors to surprising opportunities.

INFILL PROJECTS

Infill projects refer to various ways of developing an area. One well-known example is tearing down an old building in an urban core and constructing something new in its place. Another approach is purchasing an oversized lot with a house on it and dividing the lot to build on the unused portion. The existing house can either be sold or kept as a rental property.

For instance, we were once approached by someone buying an old bungalow in an urban core to flip it. The old house had a double lot, and he asked us if we would be interested in purchasing the empty part if he divided it. It was a great opportunity, and we agreed. The lot, after being separated, was small, but we could still build a duplex with two bedrooms in each unit. We got a good deal on the lot as it was off-market, and the seller needed to ensure he had a buyer in place before going through with the purchase and the severance process (see below). It was a win-win situation for both parties.

SEVERANCES

Severance refers to dividing a piece of land into smaller portions. Occasionally, you may encounter a large plot of land that would be too expensive to develop a small multi-unit property on. In such cases, you could consider dividing the land and selling pieces to offset the purchase price while retaining a portion for yourself to build on.

However, you absolutely need to consult with the municipality, land surveyors and engineers before making any purchases. There may be rules and regulations governing property severance which may make severing the property difficult, if not impossible. Note that this approach can also carry certain risks because obtaining severance approval may require environmental studies and other assessments, which can be costly and challenging.

PLANNING DEPARTMENTS AND AUCTIONS

Contact local planning and zoning departments for information on upcoming development areas and potential land deals. People who work for municipalities especially in the construction and planning departments are typically very well aware of most projects happening around town and of who owns what. They see and hear things during inspections, from neighboring complaints, and often directly from the horse's mouth. Let them know that you are seeking to do investment builds and leaving business cards with them can help. You could also ask them if there are any government programs or grants that may offer land at a discount for specific types of development or how to get information on Foreclosure and Tax Sales. You could perhaps attend foreclosure auctions and tax lien sales, where land may be available at lower prices.

DRIVING FOR DOLLARS & TARGETED MAIL

This is my least favorite method and the one I would do only if I'm really desperate. We've never had to do this yet, but maybe it works best in different markets. The goal is to drive around target areas and explore neighborhoods to look for vacant or underutilized land. Take note of "For Sale" signs and contact the owners. Look for potential. Land that might not be listed but appears neglected or vacant. Research the owner's contact information through public records and reach out. You can send letters or postcards to landowners in the areas where you're interested in purchasing land. Highlight your interest in buying and the benefits of selling directly to you. Then follow up regularly to increase the chances of a response. I just find this method time consuming and annoying.

TOP THREE TAKEAWAYS:

1. **The Hidden Costs of Raw Land Development**: Unlike serviced lots, raw land comes with zoning hurdles, environmental studies, and infrastructure costs that can delay projects for years. Our 2.8-acre project proved just how unpredictable this process can be. If you're new to development, raw land isn't the easiest starting point and I don't recommend it—it requires experience, deep pockets, and patience.

2. **Why Serviced Lots Save Time and Money**: With utilities and infrastructure already in place, serviced lots let you hit the ground running. They help avoid massive upfront costs, delays, and unexpected roadblocks, making them a safer, more predictable option—especially if you're looking for efficiency and faster returns.

3. **Finding the Best Land Deals**: The best deals aren't always on MLS. Networking, social media, and word-of-mouth can open doors to off-market opportunities. Keeping your name out there—whether through investment groups, direct outreach, or local connections—can lead to unexpected, high-value finds.

CHAPTER 8

ANALYZING A POTENTIAL LAND DEAL

B efore you ever put in an offer on a piece of land, you need to know exactly what you're getting into. A bad land deal can stall your project, drain your budget, or even force you to walk away entirely. That's why due diligence isn't just important — it's non-negotiable.

When we analyze a lot for a potential multi-unit build, we run through a specific checklist every time. It's not glamorous, but it's what saves us from expensive surprises later on. Here are the key elements we always look into:

1. **Services**

2. **Soil Tests**

3. **Easements**

4. **Zoning**

5. **Pre-consultation**

6. **Consulting the Pros**

7. **Financing**

Each of these can make or break a deal. So let's break them down — starting with the very first thing we always verify: the available services on site.

1. SERVICES

The availability of essential services is one of the most crucial considerations when analyzing a land deal. Services such as municipal water, sewage systems, electricity, and internet significantly impact the feasibility and cost of your project. Without access to these, alternative solutions may be possible, but they often require additional resources, planning, and expense. You have to fully understand the implications of missing services before purchasing the land.

For instance, start by checking if municipal water is available. If it isn't, you'll have to explore the types of wells that could be installed in your area that could supply adequate water supply to your build. Personally, we don't build multi units using wells. If the land doesn't have municipal water, we won't purchase the land since bringing in the water or installing wells is too challenging for multi-units and not a viable option here.

Another crucial aspect to consider is the sewer system. Is the land serviced by the municipal sewage system? While installing a septic field is not out of the question for us, we do need to know the soil quality in the area before agreeing to it. This can have a significant impact on the cost and complexity of the system. There's also the question of maintenance that comes with having private septic systems. Some septic models require yearly inspections that can cost a few hundred dollars each time. It's just one more thing for you to consider with a tenanted property.

You should also verify the availability of other utilities like electricity, internet, and maybe natural gas — if that's the preferred method of heating in that area. Ideally, you may want to look for a lot that has these services, and don't forget to consider the cost of upgrading the electric grid, if necessary. For example, in the case of a multi-unit build, you often need to update the electric grid to accommodate the extra units. Try calling the local electrical provider in the early planning stages to see if they can provide an estimate, or at least an idea of the scope of work required. Upgrading the grid can be expensive. Consult with your on-site electrician as well since you'll need to know if you're connecting to the grid from wires that are above or below ground.

Cautionary tale:

We have a friend who ran into a major issue with the electric grid on his first build. He was constructing a fourplex, with approved plans and permits in hand. The foundation was poured, and the trusses and joists were scheduled for delivery when the utility company arrived on-site to prepare their report on the scope of work required. That's when they pointed out high-voltage wires running above the far-right side of his property—and informed him of a mandatory ten-foot setback easement on either side of those lines.

The problem? His foundation wall was directly beneath the wires. He had no choice but to demolish that entire side, redesign the building, and scale it down to a triplex so that the foundation no longer ran within that easement. On top of the redesign costs, he lost the original trusses and joists and had to reorder a new set.

As expected, this ended up in court, with engineers, surveyors, and the city all pointing fingers at one another. However, most professionals protect themselves by stating in their contracts that the general contractor (GC) is ultimately responsible for verifying all site conditions before construction begins.

Honestly though, I'm not sure anything could have been done differently to avoid a situation like this. Perhaps it was a lack of experience from the contractor's part, but this is why he relied on the pros. I think mostly it was just one of those things that went unnoticed from all the people involved. Perhaps if he met with his electrician on-site in the early stage to discuss the service connection, the electrician would have noticed the wires and flagged it. Which is why I think that may be the best approach when you're new in construction and feeling unsure about the process of certain things. Arrange to meet the pros on site early on and try to get them to address any issue they may notice.

Another cautionary tale:

When we were building our first sixplex, we realized early on that there was no internet provider servicing the property—despite thinking we had verified this in advance. The Bell sales team initially assured us there would be no issue getting internet to the building. But once construction was underway, their technicians informed us that the service line actually stopped just before our lot, and extending it would cost $30,000.

We looked into another provider located just down the road, near their telecom shelter, assuming they could service us instead. No luck. Turns out, all the internet companies relied on Bell's infrastructure, and since Bell didn't reach our site, no one else could either.

This was a serious problem. No tenant wants to live in a unit without internet access—and it could have completely tanked the value of the property.

Thankfully, a local tech company and friend came to the rescue. He walked us through how to wire the building properly: each unit would have its own modem, connected to a centralized hub in one of the units, which would in turn link to a Starlink dish on the roof. Crisis averted.

He even set us up with firewalls and all the back-end tech we didn't fully understand. We decided to include internet in the rent and raised it by only $40 per month. It's been working great so far.

Moral of the story, make doubly sure the internet is fully available. However, I really don't hate setting up the internet this way. It stops tenants from making holes in the floors and walls from installing their own service, and it allows you to raise the rent. Making your numbers look more appealing to the bank. It doesn't have to be serviced from Starlink either, this set up can be serviced from any of the internet providers. Just make sure you have a good tech company that can set this up for you and maintain it when needed.

2. SOIL TESTS

Soil tests are extremely important. They provide essential information about the soil's composition and characteristics, helping you make informed decisions about construction and land use. I recommend a soil test as a condition in your offer to purchase. You can consult with local septic designers or excavation companies to gather information about the soil in the area before agreeing to purchase, but the best practice is to conduct a proper soil test on the land before you buy. Here's what you need to know about soil tests.

They serve several purposes, including:

1. Foundation design: Understanding the soil's load-bearing capacity is vital for designing stable and safe foundations for buildings.

2. Site suitability: Soil tests can determine if the land is suitable for construction or if additional preparations, such as soil stabilization, are necessary.

3. Environmental impact: Soil tests assess the soil's contamination level, ensuring compliance with environmental regulations and protecting public health.

4. Drainage and water management: Knowledge of the soil's permeability helps plan effective drainage systems, preventing water-related issues during and after construction.

There are various types of soil tests, each providing specific insights:

1. Soil bearing tests: This involves drilling holes in the ground using an excavator and extracting soil samples at different depths. It helps identify the soil's composition, consistency, and bearing capacity.

2. Percolation test: This assesses the soil's ability to absorb water, which is essential for septic system design and stormwater management.

3. Soil contamination test: This identifies the presence of pollutants or hazardous substances in the soil, essential for safety and environmental compliance.

We typically do a soil boring test, which only costs us about $300, by hiring a geotechnical engineer. This is usually all that's required from the city for a small residential project. Anything that's larger or commercial will need more comprehensive testing, and that's something you'll need to discuss with your municipality and engineering team, and it may also be requirements from your lender.

That said, even with positive soil test results, you're never fully in the clear until excavation begins. A boring test only samples specific points, meaning unstable soil, organic material, or old fill could still exist elsewhere on the site. Soil conditions can vary dramatically, and unexpected issues like a high water table, weak compaction, or buried debris might only become apparent once the entire footprint is exposed. In some cases, you may still need to reinforce certain areas before proceeding with construction. Once, at the beginning of another sixplex build, we had to bring in about three or four feet of rocks covering the entire surface of the dug out footprint. It cost us an extra 20k. Having a contingency plan for soil-related surprises is always a smart move.

3. EASEMENTS

As I explained in my cautionary tale earlier, you need to verify the presence of easements before purchasing a property. Easements come in various forms, but in essence, they grant someone else the legal right to use or access a portion of your land. For instance, a farmer behind your property may have the right to use a path across your lot to access the road, or a high-voltage power line overhead could restrict building within a certain distance.

Detecting easements can be tricky. Many are indicated on survey plans, so obtaining a current survey before purchasing is highly beneficial. However, not all easements are visibly marked, which is why a title search is also essential. Your lawyer will verify any registered easements before closing, as these remain with the property regardless of ownership. Additionally, your real estate agent can inquire with the seller or check their realtor database for related information. If you're dealing with utility easements, municipal or utility company records may also provide insight.

4. ZONING

Understanding the permitted uses of the property is vital. For example, if you plan to build a two-unit structure, you must verify if the zoning allows for this kind of construction. You should also know the local terminology used to describe a two-unit building. For example, a duplex (here it is considered to be two units stacked one on top of the other) or a semi-detached dwelling (here it is considered to be two units connected side-by-side). Furthermore, you must determine the property set-back requirements (the required distances between the building's footprint and each property line), the height restrictions, and the minimum lot size for each permitted use. See the following pages for an example of a zoning grid.

6.5   Village Residential First Density (RV1) Zone

No person shall hereafter use any lands, nor erect, alter, enlarge or use any building or structure in a Village Residential First Density (RV1) Zone except in accordance with the provisions of this Section and of any other relevant Sections of this By-law.

6.5.1 Permitted Uses

Residential Uses
- *Detached dwelling*
- *Duplex dwelling*
- *Linked detached dwelling*
- *Semi-detached dwelling*
- *Group home (1)*
- *Retirement home (1)*

Accessory Residential Uses
- *Bed and breakfast (1)(2)*
- *Home-based business, Village (2)*
- *Lodging house (1)(2)(3)*
- *Private home day care (1)(2)*
- *Second unit (4)*
- *Short-term rental*

Institutional and Community Uses
- *Emergency service facility*

Open Space Uses
- *Community garden*
- *Conservation use*
- *Park, public*
- *Stormwater management facility*

Additional Regulations for Permitted Uses

(1) The maximum number of private bedrooms or living units, for uses listed under footnote (1), shall be 4.
(2) A maximum of one of the uses subject to footnote (2) shall be permitted in a *dwelling*.
(3) The maximum number of *lodging units*, for uses subject to footnote (3), shall be 4.
(4) Second units are subject to the provisions of section 4.41.

6.5.2 Zone Requirements

The zone requirements for *lots* in a Village Residential First Density (RV1) Zone are set out in Table 6.5.2, below.

Table 6.5.2: Zone requirements in the Village Residential First Density (RV1) Zone				
	Detached dwelling, Group Home, Retirement Home	Semi-detached dwelling	Duplex dwelling	Linked dwelling
Minimum *lot area* - Entirely serviced on private services	2,500.0 m²	1,250.0 m² / DU	2,500.0 m²	1,250.0 m² / DU
Minimum *lot frontage on private services*	38.0 m	19.0 m / DU	38.0 m	38.0 m
Minimum *lot area* - Partial service (water)	1,300.0 m²	900.0 m² / DU	1,800.0 m²	1,300.0 m²
Minimum *lot frontage on partial services*	22.5 m	15.0 m / DU	30.0 m	30.0 m
Minimum *front yard*				
- Local Road	7.5 m			
- County Road	10.0 m			
Minimum *exterior side yard*				
- Local Road	6.0 m			
- County Road	10.0 m			
Minimum *interior side yard*	1.5 m (1)			
Minimum *rear yard*	6.0 m			
Minimum *dwelling unit area*	100.0 m²			
Maximum *building height*	11.0 m			
Maximum *Lot Coverage*	30%			

Additional Requirements for Zone Requirements Table 6.5.2

(1) If a *semi-detached dwelling* or *linked dwelling* is severed, the zone requirements continue to apply to the original *lot* except that the *interior side yard* requirement does not apply along the common *lot line*.

TIP: Required "yards" or setbacks are the areas that lie between a property line and the structure. It basically means the unbuildable area. They keep houses from being built too close to each other or too close to the roads.

A front yard setback is the requirement for how far the front of the building needs to be set from the front lot line. An exterior side yard setback is the requirement that applies to a corner lot, on the side of the house abutting a street. An interior side yard setback is the requirement for how far the building needs to be from the side lot line and the rear yard setback is the requirement for how far the building needs to be from the rear lot line

Ideally, the township or municipality you're considering will have a modern and interactive city map that will include helpful information on each piece of property. These maps usually include the ability to search online for an address, click on a link, and view the available services, lot size, zoning with a link to the zoning bylaw, flood zone status, assessment value, and more. If your township lacks this feature, don't worry. You can still obtain the information you need by contacting the municipality and asking if they can provide the zoning bylaw and, if available, an old survey. Just make sure to ask the right questions. This brings me to my next point...

5. PRE-CONSULTATION

The next step in purchasing a property is to request a pre-consultation meeting with the municipality. You will usually do this after you check off some or all of the above-mentioned steps and feel more confident that you found a good deal. You can include a condition in your offer to purchase that the results of the pre-consultation meeting must meet your satisfaction. A knowledgeable realtor can help you word this in a way that protects your interests, allowing you to walk away from the deal if necessary.

I recommend sending an email and having an in-person meeting with the municipality. Start by emailing the zoning department, detailing your plans for the property, and inquiring about any potential issues. That email is valuable because it will provide you with a written record of the conversation.

For larger or more complex projects, it may also be necessary for you to have a personal meeting where you can discuss the project in more detail. Be sure to request a written summary of the meeting, or write one yourself and send it to everyone involved via email to ensure you have all the information you need and to make sure that everything that was discussed is documented. Do the same with phone calls... trust me, document *everything*. I have severe trust issues when it comes to city officials unfortunately, based on *several* issues in the past.

Here's a list of example questions to ask them:

- ☐ Would you support this project?
- ☐ What problems do you think we would have in getting our permit request
- ☐ approved?
- ☐ Can you provide a list of things we need to have done?
- ☐ Can you also provide a list of local vendors and trades to help us accomplish those tasks?
- ☐ Can I get a rough estimate of how much the permit/development fee would cost? Here in Ontario, our new construction permits are crazy expensive. Example: $55,000 for a semi-detached (side-by-side duplex).
- ☐ How long does it usually take to process an application of this type?
- ☐ If I need to demolish a building, what do I need to apply for a demolition permit and what is the demolition process? (In some places, you need to have your new build permit approved before being granted a demolition permit. If you need to demolish, make sure it's not a heritage property.)
- ☐ What is the process for a zoning change or minor variance [or other approvals]? (I'll talk about these in Chapter 9, but you should still ask the city to clearly explain the process, the fees, and what is needed for those to be approved.)

6. CONSULTING THE PROS

Depending on the type of project and what services I'll need for a build, I like to consult with local professionals. This may include a land surveyor, excavator contractor, civil engineer, electrician, or other professionals. My goal is to gain as much knowledge as possible about the soil conditions, site preparation, and permit approval process. My doing so can avoid any unpleasant surprises during the building process. This step is comparable to avoiding potential pitfalls by peeling back the layers of an old home that's being renovated. These professionals can provide detailed insights and recommendations, ensuring you are well-prepared and informed before starting the construction process.

7. FINANCING

Finally, verify that you can obtain financing for your intended building project. Like I've said before, always include financing as another condition in your purchase offer. Securing financing early in the process ensures you have the necessary funds to proceed with the project without delays. Taking tips from Chapter 5, consult with banks or financial institutions to explore your financing options, and consider the impact of interest rates and loan terms on your project's budget. A well-structured financing plan provides financial stability and confidence as you move forward with your multi-unit build.

TOP THREE TAKEAWAYS:

1. **Essential Services Availability**: Before purchasing land for a multi-unit build, ensure that essential services such as municipal water, sewer systems, electricity, internet, and possibly natural gas are available. Lack of these services can significantly impact the feasibility and cost of the project. For example, without municipal water, a multi-unit build may not be viable as a well may not provide adequate water supply. Additionally, upgrading existing utility infrastructure, like the electric grid, can be costly and should be considered early in the planning stages.

2. **Soil Tests and Zoning Requirements**: Conducting soil tests is crucial to understand the soil's load-bearing capacity, contamination levels, and drainage properties. These tests inform foundation design, environmental compliance, and water management plans. Similarly, verifying zoning requirements and property set-backs is essential to ensure the intended construction is permissible. This includes understanding local terminologies for building types, height restrictions, and minimum lot sizes. These steps help avoid costly legal and construction issues down the line.

3. **Pre-consultation with Municipality**: Request a pre-consultation meeting with the municipality after preliminary checks on services, soil tests, and zoning. This meeting helps identify any potential issues with permit approvals and provides a clear path forward. Questions about project support, potential problems, required tasks, local vendors, permit fees, and processing times should be asked. This step ensures that you have all necessary information and written records to protect your interests, and can make an informed decision about proceeding with the purchase and project.

CHAPTER 9

THE PLANNING PHASE

N ow that you have your lot, it's finally time to put your game plan in motion! The first step is to determine the best design that will fully utilize your lot's potential. This is where you would hire a drafting tech or architect. These experts have the knowledge and experience to verify zoning requirements and ensure that you maximize your property's income potential.

> TIP: Architects and architectural technologists are not the same. They are different in their education, licensing, and professional standards. Architects typically take on more commercial, larger-scale projects, have more qualifications, and have a different kind of approval stamp, so their rates are higher. In comparison, technologists are usually less expensive and tend to focus more on residential drafting, with perhaps some small commercial projects. Inquire with your municipality about what is required for your project and whom they can recommend. Hint: Rob and I are technologists, and it's all you need here for small multi-family dwellings. Architects tend to be too bougie for us.

I'm going to use the term "draftsman" to describe the one doing the architectural drawings. Using the two-unit example from the zoning information in the previous chapter, your draftsman can help you determine if you can build semi-detached units or if you need to stack your units to create an up-and-down duplex. Your designer can find an effective way to tailor the space for adding a unit in the basement, or for building up if that is a better option. They will ensure your plans comply with local bylaws regarding parking spaces, zoning setbacks, green space requirements, and more.

At this stage, you need to consider the sufficient number of parking spaces per unit and whether each unit will have balconies or outdoor areas. Voicing your preferences to the designer early on will allow them to plan the space accordingly. I talk about designing later in this chapter, but you should emphasize that you want a functional and budget-friendly build. You don't need excessive features like high ceilings or complex roof designs unless that's what you really want. For long-term rentals, simple yet attractive designs tend to appeal to a broader range of renters. Choose materials that are commonly used and easy to find; that way, you don't run into any delays due to shortages, shipping, or unavailability of specialized trades.

It's at this time of the early design stage that you and your designer would determine if a minor variance application, zoning change, or other type of application would be feasible options for your project.

MINOR VARIANCE APPLICATIONS

A minor variance involves seeking relief from a specific zoning bylaw that's constraining your project. In simpler terms, it's asking for an exception to a zoning rule so your project can proceed. For example, if you want to build a duplex on a lot that's 36 metres wide instead of the required 38 metres, you could apply to the Committee of Adjustment for an exemption.

The process can take time, depending on your municipality's procedures, and usually involves application fees. You'll likely need to submit a survey plan, preliminary site plans, elevations, floor plans, a cover letter explaining your request, and proof of ownership. Including 3D renderings can help the committee and neighbours visualize the project. If your draftsman doesn't include renderings or if his fee is too high for that, you can usually find a virtual 3D specialist through social media or Upwork that can get one done for you quickly and at a low or manageable rate.

The application is reviewed at a committee meeting, which may occur infrequently (once a month in our town), potentially causing delays. Once the meeting is scheduled, signs are posted on the property, and letters are sent to neighbouring properties. Neighbours with concerns can voice them at the meeting or submit them in writing. However, the committee only considers valid concerns when making decisions.

If the committee finds no major issues, they'll grant pre-approval. There's usually an appeal period before full approval is granted. Predicting the outcome can be difficult, as it depends on the specifics of the project and any concerns raised by neighbours. Some applications go through several rounds of revisions and take months, or even longer, to be approved. While others are approved on the first try.

For a minor exemption, like a two-metre width reduction, chances of approval are typically good, as it's unlikely to cause significant impact. However, there's no way to guarantee approval before purchasing the land. Consulting with a city planner during a pre-consultation meeting can provide useful insights, though it may still require taking a calculated risk.

ZONING CHANGES

This type of application can be trickier and more complex than a minor variance. This process is considered a bigger deal because you are requesting to change the official amendment plan and the zoning bylaw. You'll need to get approval from not only the municipality, but also higher government organizations like a ministry or county (or those applicable in your area). We have done a couple of these so far, one was super simple and straightforward. One took about three to four months from the time of application to receiving full approval. Then another that took longer when counting for the preparation work before we applied, about nine months in total. However, that was more specific to the project itself and the municipality's requirements.

We had requested the zoning to change from commercial to residential for a 48-unit development (24 units for us and 24 units for our friend who owns the lot adjacent to us). Most commercial spaces and retail stores in that town were sitting empty and for sale, so the committee recognized that it was in the city's best interest to approve the change to attract more residents and potentially bring back retail stores. To ensure a smooth process, we hired a planning consultant and had an official pre-consultation with the municipality. This allowed all the relevant departments and organizations to review the project proposal. Additionally, we hired a civil engineering firm to complete a preliminary hydrogeological study and terrain analysis, as well as guide us through a meeting with the Ministry of the Environment, which was necessary due to the requirement for large, communal septic fields.

We presented our case to the committee with all the necessary reports and documentation, including a ten-page application form and a 22-page planning rationale detailing the project, prepared by our consultant. After a discussion in which we answered many questions, and there was a vote in favour of the change, the application went through an adoption hearing, an appeal process, and finally, a final adoption notice. The application fees alone totalled over $10,000, not including the cost of engineering and consultation.

It is also important to note that, due to the commercial zoning of the lot, the bank was not willing to finance our lot until after the zoning was successfully changed. Even then, they only offered us 50 percent of the financing and a higher interest rate. We had to make alternative arrangements and purchased the lot outright. We only got our money back once the first phase of the project was done (a sixplex) and got our mortgage for the building.

BUILDING METHODS

When building a house or a small-scale residential project in North America, there are several common construction methods to consider. Each method has its advantages and drawbacks, so let's take a closer look at some of the most widely used options:

1. **Traditional Stick-Framing** is a construction method where a building's skeleton is constructed on-site using individual pieces of dimensional lumber, such as 2x4s or 2x6s. This method

involves assembling walls, floors, and roof structures piece by piece, typically relying on a platform-framing technique where each story is built on top of the one below.

- **Pros:** This is the most common and cost-effective method of building, especially for single-family homes and small multi-unit projects. It's widely understood by contractors and municipalities, making permits and financing straightforward.

- **Cons:** While affordable, it offers less insulation and energy efficiency compared to newer methods, and it may not be as durable in extreme weather conditions.

2. **Modular Construction** is a building method where structures are constructed off-site in factory-controlled environments as individual modules or sections. These modules are then transported to the building site and assembled into a finished structure.

- **Pros:** The process allows for faster construction timelines, consistent quality, and reduced material waste. Modular construction is often used for residential, commercial, and industrial buildings, offering flexibility in design while leveraging the efficiency of mass production.

- **Cons:** Despite these benefits, modular construction faces challenges with local building codes, zoning regulations, and financing. Anything that is unfamiliar and outside traditional methods can complicate approval processes. Also, if the site is tight and lacks space to set down the modules and the crane it might make the assembly complicated.

3. **Prefab** (short for prefabricated construction) refers to building components that are manufactured off-site in a controlled environment, and then transported to the construction site for assembly. These components can range from entire modular units to smaller elements like wall panels or trusses.

- **Pros:** improves efficiency, reduces on-site labor, and minimizes construction timelines. Prefabs also tend to have less material waste.

- **Cons:** Transportation and assembly logistics can add unexpected costs or problems, and customization may be limited compared to traditional builds. Also, if you have a tight site in an urban area with limited space, you might not have room to bring in the prefab walls as well as the crane during assembly. We did two sixplexes in pre-fab walls, but only because the sites were big enough and we had enough room to make the assembly go smoothly. The framing company was not comfortable doing the same thing on our triplex site that was too tight in an urban area.

4. **Insulated Concrete Forms (ICFs)**
    Insulated Concrete Forms (ICF) are hollow, interlocking blocks made of rigid foam that are stacked and filled with concrete.

    - **Pros:** ICF construction provides excellent insulation, energy efficiency, and durability. It's also resistant to natural disasters like storms or fires, and reduces noise transmission between units—a big plus for multi-unit buildings.

    - **Cons:** The main drawback is cost. ICF can increase your total project costs by about 30 percent compared to traditional wood framing, and it's not always clear whether you'll recoup that investment in property value or savings.

5. **Structural Insulated Panels (SIPs)**
    Structural Insulated Panels (SIP) are prefabricated building panels consisting of an insulating foam core sandwiched between two structural boards.

    - **Pros:** SIPs offer great energy efficiency, strength for walls, roofs and floors, and reduce construction time due to their prefab nature.

    - **Cons:** They can be more expensive upfront, may require specialized contractors for installation, and can have limited flexibility for future modifications or changes to the building's layout.

6. **Concrete Block Construction**

   Concrete block construction uses stacked concrete masonry units (CMUs), bonded with mortar for residential and commercial buildings.

   - **Pros:** They provide durability, fire resistance, and strength, especially in harsh weather environments. They're also excellent for soundproofing.

   - **Cons:** Concrete block construction can be labor-intensive, have a slower build time compared to other methods, and may require additional insulation or finishing to improve energy efficiency and aesthetics.

7. **Timber Frame Construction**

   Timber frame construction uses a framework of heavy wooden posts and beams, joined with traditional or modern fasteners, to create a strong, open-structured building with minimal need for interior load-bearing walls.

   - **Pros:** Timber framing creates visually stunning homes with exposed beams and a unique design. It's also durable and can be quite energy efficient with proper insulation.

   - **Cons:** Is more expensive, requires ongoing maintenance to prevent issues like rot or pests, and may have limitations in fire resistance unless treated with fire-retardant materials.

8. **Precast Concrete**

   Precast concrete construction involves manufacturing concrete components off-site in a controlled environment, then transporting and assembling them on-site.

   - **Pros:** Ensures consistent quality and reduces on-site construction time. They are durable and energy-efficient.

   - **Cons:** Higher upfront costs, transportation challenges, and limited design flexibility.

9. **Steel Frame Construction**

   Steel frame construction uses a skeleton of steel columns and beams. Typically used for commercial builds.

- **Pros:** Steel is durable, fire-resistant, and can be prefabricated to speed up construction. It's also great for larger buildings where strength is a primary concern.

- **Cons:** Steel framing is more expensive than wood and may require additional insulation due to its poor thermal performance.

Although there are numerous construction methods available, we've consistently chosen traditional woof framing for our projects. Why? Primarily to avoid disrupting our established systems. Our approach is about balancing quality, speed, and cost-effectiveness. With stick-framing, we know the process, the costs are predictable, and both financial institutions and municipalities are familiar with this method. Experimenting with other methods could derail our systems, jeopardize our project timelines, and ultimately affect our investment goals.

The only method we tried, which still fell in the box of stick framing, was pre-framing all the walls of our sixplexes in the warehouse ahead of time. Basically this meant that we shipped all the wood for the walls at the framer's warehouse, they framed every exterior and interior wall indoors while the excavation and foundation was being prepared on site. Then when it's time to frame, the crews just need to frame the floors on site. They transport the walls and use the crane to bring them on the floors, and place them all in place. The cost was the same as framing on site, but the goal was to speed up the process. Plus, it allows the crews to frame indoors and the project to continue even during bad weather.

In theory it's a great idea, just as long as your framing crew is able to stick to the schedule and offer these services to fit the budget.

BUILDING "GREEN"

PRACTICAL APPROACHES FOR SMALL-SCALE RENTALS

Going green doesn't have to mean going overboard. If you're building small-scale multi-unit properties, incorporating sustainable practices can be surprisingly simple — and often just comes down to making smarter choices as you go. You don't have to do everything, but by focusing on a few key areas, you can make a big difference in efficiency, longevity, and appeal.

ENERGY-EFFICIENT DESIGN: KEEP IT SMART AND SIMPLE

Some people swear by orienting buildings to capture natural sunlight. And while that sounds great in theory (especially if you studied architecture like I did), it doesn't always make a noticeable impact in rental buildings. Tenants aren't necessarily choosing their units based on where the sun hits at 10 a.m.

Instead, keep things focused on what actually matters long-term: a space-efficient layout and solid building envelope. This means things like high-quality insulation (even doubling up in key areas), well-sealed windows and doors, and maybe even triple-pane glass if your climate calls for it. These are the decisions that will impact comfort, energy use, and utility bills for years to come.

ENERGY-EFFICIENT SYSTEMS: EASY WINS THAT LAST

Swapping out traditional bulbs for LEDs is a no-brainer. They last longer, use less energy, and cost basically the same now. The same goes for choosing Energy Star-rated appliances — they're widely available and make a noticeable dent in energy usage.

Programmable thermostats are also a great addition, especially in common areas or units with fluctuating occupancy. And when it comes to HVAC, look into high-efficiency options like a dual electric heat pump and A/C combo, or a natural gas furnace with a decent SEER rating. Heat Recovery Ventilators (HRVs) are another smart upgrade if you're looking to improve air quality and reduce heat loss. HRVs are even a code requirement here for most HVAC systems.

I go into a bit more HVAC detail in Chapter 13, but just know that these system upgrades are some of the lowest-effort, highest-impact changes you can make.

SUSTAINABLE MATERIALS: USE WHAT MAKES SENSE

If you want to take it a step further, consider using recycled or reclaimed materials. One example: we once used rigid insulation boards that had been removed from a commercial roof replacement. They were in perfect shape, but the roofing crew had to replace them anyway as part of the job. Score for us!

Locally sourced materials are also a great choice when available — not only does this reduce the carbon footprint from transportation, but it can also support businesses in your area. And if you're using wood, look into FSC-certified products to ensure it's coming from responsibly managed forests.

WATER EFFICIENCY: AN EASY WIN

Low-flow toilets, faucets, and showerheads are surprisingly efficient these days — and most people won't even notice the difference in performance. If you're looking to go a bit further, rainwater harvesting systems can help with irrigation or other non-potable uses, especially on larger lots. It's not something we've implemented widely, but it's on our radar for future builds with more outdoor space.

RENEWABLE ENERGY: SOLAR'S STILL WORTH CONSIDERING

Solar is one of those things that sounds intimidating, but can actually pay off when done right. We've installed panels on our personal home, and it cut our electric bill down to a fraction. We considered doing it for some of our fourplexes, especially the ones with full sun exposure — but recent changes to government rebates made it less appealing for now.

If you're considering it for a rental, just make sure to:

- Do a solar feasibility study.
- Ask about net metering with your local utility.
- Install separate meters to track production and consumption.
- Include a lease addendum to clarify that tenants still pay for their own usage (while benefiting from lower bills).

You could also look into a Power Purchase Agreement (PPA) or a solar lease if you're trying to offset the upfront costs.

One note: be mindful of things like snow or ice sliding off panels in winter. It's a real hazard in colder climates and should be factored into both your design and your insurance.

SMART HOME TECH: COOL, BUT MAYBE NOT WORTH IT

Smart thermostats, lighting systems, and energy apps are definitely trendy — but they're not always necessary in rentals. In our case, we try to avoid things that add more servicing or tech issues for tenants (or ourselves). That said, motion sensors or programmable systems in common areas can be helpful and pretty hands-off once installed.

If you go down the smart home path, keep it simple and make sure tenants won't need to call you every time their app logs out.

EFFICIENT LANDSCAPING: SET IT AND FORGET IT

Choosing native plants and drought-resistant greenery can cut down on watering, lower your maintenance time, and still look great. It's something we're moving toward more and more — especially in areas where summer heat tends to wipe out traditional landscaping.

You can also consider using permeable paving materials for walkways and driveways. These allow rainwater to absorb into the ground naturally, which helps reduce runoff and supports local water systems.

FINAL THOUGHTS ON GOING GREEN

I know — it might seem like these are small tweaks. But they add up. Choosing to build "green-ish" doesn't have to be complicated or expensive. You don't need to do it all at once, and you don't need to be perfect. Even implementing one or two of these strategies can have a positive long-term impact on your rental's performance, your maintenance load, and yes — the environment.

Sustainability isn't just good for the planet. In the long run, it's good business too.

DESIGNING INTERIOR SPACES

A few things we tend to consider when designing the interior spaces of our units include the following:

- Designing private entrances for each unit and avoiding common hallways or spaces whenever possible, as they're extra maintenance and costs that we can avoid. We also try to include private mechanical rooms for each unit, with direct access to the units' electrical panels, heat and water sources.

- Including individual laundry rooms in each unit. We do this for the tenant's convenience and also as it raises the rent value. Especially since our town here isn't big enough to have a public laundromat. We also see the appeal of having communal laundry rooms inside the building with coin-operated machines for extra income, especially in bigger multi-units.

- Including enough closets and storage spaces like an entrance closet, a linen closet, sometimes even a pantry, a walk-in closet in the master bedroom, and an extra closet for storage if there's room. Outdoor sheds are also an opportunity for extra income if you want to charge extra to include those.

- Designing the master bedrooms to be big enough to fit a king-size bed, as this is a question I would get often when I showed units.

- Consider work spaces when possible.

- Including, if possible, a double vanity if there's only one bathroom in the unit.

- Trying to include enough cabinet space in the kitchen, and a pantry where possible.

- Installing large windows and wide patio doors for lots of natural lighting.

- Strategically placing windows on the side of neighbouring properties for optimal privacy. One of the advantages of building new, you get to plan ahead and choose how you want to avoid your neighbors.

- Considering patio doors with integrated blinds in the windowpanes. Tenants wouldn't need to put up curtains over the larger openings, and it would minimize the amount of patching at turnovers.

- Designing certain units of the build to have access to a garage really increases the rentability of a rental. People absolutely love having garages and it can dramatically increase the rent value of a unit. We try to incorporate garages when we can. Usually we design them so the main floor units have direct access and therefore those units will pay more in rent. You can also consider doing something like a large shared garage detached from the building if there's room on the land, but then you need to make sure that the leases are ironclad about sharing the space, the maintenance, the liability, and other details. Or you could do one large garage with individual compartments. Like at our sixplex where there will be multiple construction phases on the land, we plan on building one long and narrow garage with individual compartments in it. There won't be enough garage bays for each tenant but those who really want one can pay the extra (possibly 300$ or more) a month for one.

Try to place yourself in the renter's shoes and think of the little details you would appreciate having in your home. Remain mindful of the costs, ease of maintenance down the line, and long-term appeal to compete against other available units. Ultimately, it still has to make sense, and it comes down to making the numbers work (add on value vs. costs vs. financing) and finding what works best for your rental market.

DESIGNING EXTERIOR SPACES

It's important to include exterior spaces for each unit in multi-unit developments. Providing a space for fresh air and outdoor activities such as barbecuing can increase tenant satisfaction and tenancy length. This has become even more important since the Covid-19 pandemic, as outdoor space has become a top priority for a lot of renters. Exterior spaces can also be greatly beneficial to tenants with pets, assuming pets are allowed. To address this, we aim to design buildings with private balconies or designated outdoor spaces for each unit. We have a couple buildings with shared yards, and we found that managing a shared yard can be demanding and result in more turnover and maintenance issues.

However, managing outdoor spaces, in general, can always be an issue as they are one more thing to look after and can even invite complaints. Nevertheless, offering any form of outdoor space can still be beneficial, even if shared. To simplify their management, we include specific terms in the lease agreement regarding maintenance and usage rules, which will be outlined in the documents provided in chapter 19: The DIY Landlord.

With respect to parking spaces, considering the needs of tenants and the local area is essential. In areas with limited pedestrian accessibility, we aim to provide two parking spaces per unit. In more urban areas, one parking space is often the norm, with an option to pay for additional parking. Insufficient parking can cause people significant inconvenience, and I've seen it often when good tenants have relocated due to this issue. With your designer, try to plan for convenient parking when you have enough space on the property and local conditions are favourable.

Finally, like I mentioned earlier, adding outdoor storage solutions such as sheds or garages can generate additional income for your property. It's worth considering if you have the space available, but be careful not to compromise the usable living space. Adding storage in addition to — not instead of — functional and rentable living space, would be the best option.

Remember, the design and construction drawings will set the tone for the building process and the building's lifespan. Choosing the right designer is important to get the results you want. See Chapter 13 to help maximize your design's efficiency.

TOP THREE TAKEAWAYS:

1. **Navigating Regulatory Approvals**: Understanding the process for minor variance applications and zoning changes is essential. Minor variances allow for flexibility in zoning bylaws, while zoning changes are more complex and require higher-level approvals. Early consultations with city planners and hiring planning consultants can streamline these processes. Be prepared for potential delays and costs associated with applications, and weigh these factors carefully before purchasing land.

2. **Modular and Prefabricated Construction Have Benefits but Come with Challenges:** While modular and prefab construction methods can speed up timelines and reduce waste, they often face obstacles like zoning restrictions, financing difficulties, and site logistics. For instance, the author successfully used prefab walls for a sixplex on a large site but found it impractical for tighter urban areas. Careful evaluation of site conditions and regulations is necessary before opting for these methods.

3. **Optimizing Design for Functionality and Cost-Efficiency**: Effective design involves considering unit layout, parking, outdoor spaces, and material choices. Emphasize functional and budget-friendly designs to appeal to a broad range of renters. Avoid unnecessary features unless they significantly enhance the property's value. Incorporating common, easily available materials can prevent delays and ensure smooth construction.

CHAPTER 10

THE POWER OF ADDITIONAL DWELLING UNITS (ADUS)

As you dive deeper into your BTR (Build-to-Rent) investment journey, you'll likely come across a range of exciting opportunities — along with an even wider range of challenges. One of the biggest headaches many investors face is rezoning. It can feel like an uphill battle: jumping through hoops, waiting weeks (or months) for hearings, and hoping for approval. Plus, you can run into problems like neighbors complaining and working against you, or the municipality flat out refusing your application.

So what then? Do you walk away from the deal? Do you lose your deposit? Do you give up on the project?

What if there was a workaround?

That's where **Additional Dwelling Units (ADUs)** come in.

An ADU is a smaller, secondary housing unit located on the same lot as a primary residence. Think: a basement apartment, a backyard suite, or a separate structure like a laneway house or garden suite.

These units are a powerful tool in your real estate arsenal because they allow you to increase rental income and property value — often without needing to go through rezoning or buy additional land. They also offer flexibility, meet housing demand, and can often be built faster than full-scale developments. For investors looking to stretch their dollar and minimize red tape, ADUs can be a game changer.

WHY YOU SHOULD CARE ABOUT ADUS

Maximizing Existing Properties: ADUs help you unlock the hidden potential of your existing lots. Say you've got a property where zoning allows only a side-by-side duplex. The next step? Verify if ADUs are permitted under that zoning. If they are — that's your golden ticket. You could add a basement suite or upper unit to each side, effectively turning your duplex into a fourplex, without a zoning battle.

Regulatory Changes and Incentives: In recent years, many cities have eased restrictions and introduced incentives for ADU development as a response to the housing crisis. This means fewer roadblocks and more green lights for investors like you. Be proactive — reach out to your city's zoning or building department and ask specific questions about what's allowed under current bylaws. You might be surprised by how much flexibility is already available.

REAL-LIFE EXAMPLE

This is the story of when we took a perfectly nice looking duplex we had built just a few years before, took the roof off, set it on the front lawn, built up an ADU and put the roof back on.

We built a Duplex from scratch in 2018 in a really good location. We had acquired the land when we were approached by someone buying an old bungalow in an urban core to flip it.

The old house had a double lot, and he asked us if we would be interested in purchasing the empty part if he divided it. It was a great opportunity, and we agreed. The lot, after being severed, was small, but we could still build a duplex with two bedrooms in each unit. This was the maximum density we could do at the time with the R1 zoning. We got a good deal on the lot for 68k as it was an off-market deal.

I don't remember our total building costs, but our final mortgage was for 302k with a 5-year fixed rate of 3.74 percent.

Fast forward to 2023, when Ontario introduced Bill 23 — legislation designed to boost housing supply by overriding local zoning restrictions. It allowed property owners to add multiple dwelling units on a single lot, even if the original zoning didn't permit it. For Build-to-Rent investors like us, this opened up huge opportunities to maximize density without lengthy rezoning processes.

Hint: It's not just in Ontario, a lot of regions have become more flexible with this sort of thing to help speed up housing development.

This duplex was one of our least cash-flowing properties. It maybe cashflowed about 300$ a month, yet it was located in a prime location. Selling it was never going to be a question, but we knew we were due to renew its mortgage rate at the end of 2023 (our 5 year term was ending) meaning we would start to lose money on it every month.

Then, the tenants residing in the top unit requested to move into another one of our bigger units that I had just posted available. This is when Rob came up with the crazy idea. He was discussing the new Bill with Isaac, our general labour, while they were working on a project next door to this duplex. They were brainstorming ways to take advantage of this bill. Rob stepped outside, looked at the roof of the duplex and said: "What if we take the roof off of this thing?" And there you go...

We knew the foundation was able to take it since it was built only five years before and it was the exact same foundation we would have poured whether it had two storeys or three. I took out my planning software, opened the original drawings and got to work designing a staircase on the main floor by moving the existing front door a foot or so to the right, eliminating the entrance closet and shrinking the entrance hall by a foot to make room for the new stairs. Rob got to work by speaking to a few framers and seeing what they thought.

Instagram post May 12, 2023:

Before

Big news alert! I'm finally able to share what we are planning with this property! We're taking this Duplex we built in 2018 and converting it into a TRIPLEX!

Listen to this: We're literally taking off the roof, putting it on the front lawn, building up a new unit, and then putting the roof back on 😳 *It sounds insane, but we're confident that we can push that ROI and value way further and create a diamond in our portfolio! This property is in a prime location and it deserves a polish.*

Our top unit tenants moved into another one of our buildings so we took the opportunity to do this now especially since this property's mortgage term will be due for renewal at the end of the year so the timing is perfect for a refinance! We've never done anything like this before so stay tuned and wish us luck!!

It took 2.5 days of sunny weather to take the roof off, frame the third level and put the roof back on.

📄 NOTE: This may not be structurally possible for every building. Consult with a structural engineer.

Our basement tenant continued to live in his unit the entire length of the project. He was really understanding and supportive about the whole thing. We did our best to minimize the impact the project had on him, but I'm sure it still wasn't easy for him.

With the new appraisal we were able to refinance and pull out a chunk, while more than doubling our monthly cashflow with this added income despite the rate hikes of 2023.

Let's talk numbers

Initial mortgage:	302,000$
Old 2018 Appraisal as a Duplex:	392,000$
The new 3rd unit monthly rent:	1,900$
New 2023 Appraisal as a Triplex:	900,000$
Mortgage balance as of time of the completed renovation:	269,000$
Renovation:	165,000$
	= 434,000$
New mortgage:	465,000$
New monthly cashflow:	1,000$

We had a budget of 150k for this project and went over budget at approx 165k. A few of the big ticket items included the framing, the crane operator and the electrical work. The framing and crane was mostly inflated due to liability seeing as no one had ever done a project like this before. We understood and we bit the bullet. Electrical work also ended up being more since we had never done something like this. It was a big job just with adding in the new service, disconnecting the main floor unit, moving the panel, etc.

The new mortgage covered all of the money we put into the project + 31k extra to put in our pockets. Could we have asked for a bigger mortgage? No, actually. Given the new interest rate and the existing lease that was rent controlled in the basement unit, we didn't qualify for more. But as long as we didn't need to leave any money in the deal and we got extra on top of it, we were happy campers! Plus, a smaller mortgage means more cashflow.

This was, without a doubt, one of my favorite projects. It was exciting to tackle something so unconventional and transform what wasn't working into something that did. We took control of the numbers. The best part was watching cars slow to a crawl, drivers craning their necks and practically stopping in the middle of the road to catch a glimpse of the roof soaring through the air, suspended by a crane.

ADU WORKAROUNDS: MAKING THE MOST OF YOUR STRATEGY

Here are three more ways to incorporate the use of these additional units:

1. **Garage Conversion:** Transforming an existing garage into an ADU can be a cost-effective and practical solution. With proper planning and design, a garage conversion can offer a comfortable living space.

2. **Above-Garage Units:** If your property features an attached garage, consider constructing an ADU above it. This method utilizes underused space and adds a separate dwelling while preserving the existing structure.

3. **Tiny Homes:** Embrace the tiny home trend by placing a detached ADU on your property. These compact living spaces are both economical and versatile and will attract tenants who are seeking a minimalist lifestyle.

KEY CONSIDERATIONS FOR ADUS

- **Local Regulations**: Each municipality has its own rules and regulations regarding ADUs. It is crucial to research and understand these before embarking on any ADU project. This includes understanding zoning laws, building codes, and any permits required. Always do your pre-consultations and *always* follow up spoken conversations in *writing*.

- **Planning and Design**: Meticulous planning is essential to the success of your ADU project. Engage with professionals such as architects, contractors, and real estate experts to ensure your ADU is both functional and attractive to potential tenants.

- **Financial Planning**: While ADUs can be a lucrative investment, it is essential to consider the costs involved, including construction, permits, and potential impact on property taxes. Ensure you have a clear financial plan and budget to avoid any unexpected expenses and make sure the costs won't outweigh the return.

- **Tenant Considerations**: ADUs can attract a diverse range of tenants, from young professionals to retirees. Understand the needs and preferences of your target market to design an ADU that will appeal to them. Consider features such as privacy, accessibility, and amenities that will make your ADU stand out in the rental market.

Before jumping into adding extra units on existing buildings, obviously you should weigh the upfront costs against the long-term return. While construction expenses, permits, and potential financing can add up, the increased rental income and property value appreciation often make the investment worthwhile. But when it comes to BTR, I think they are almost always the sure way to go. Instead of pursuing complex zoning changes, working within the existing rules is usually a lot easier—and cheaper. In the end, it's about working smart instead of working hard, with smart investments that generate strong, sustainable returns.

TOP THREE TAKEAWAYS:

1. **ADUs Are a Powerful Solution When Rezoning Isn't an Option**
Instead of getting stuck in costly and time-consuming rezoning processes, explore adding ADUs like basement suites, garden suites, or additional stories. They can significantly increase your rental income and property value — often without changing zoning.

2. **Legislation Like Ontario's Bill 23 Has Opened New Doors**
Recent regulatory shifts are making ADU additions easier than ever. Stay informed and take advantage of these changes by speaking with your local building department — what wasn't possible a few years ago might be totally doable now.

3. **Creative Design + Strategic Execution = Game-Changing Results**
Our roof-lift ADU project more than doubled our cashflow and left us with money in the bank. With careful planning, good timing, and the right team, even unconventional ideas can produce big wins — without adding new land or starting from scratch.

CHAPTER 11

THE CONSTRUCTION BUDGET

You might be thinking, "Shouldn't we have discussed the budget earlier, like when we were talking about the appraisal and financing?" Well, not exactly. A little, maybe—but mostly no.

Here's why: you can't fully plan your budget until you know exactly what you're building. First, you need to secure the land, because the purchase price is a key part of your overall costs. But that's just the start. The land you choose will determine available services, zoning regulations, the number of units you can build, site constraints, and essentially everything else you need to know about your project. However, you must first address the financing to determine how much you can be approved for and if you're even in a position to shop for land. That's why we had to cover those topics first.

Only after securing financing pre-approval and the land can you begin planning the building. Once the design is nearly finalized—including all amenities and systems—you can create a complete and accurate budget. Until then, you're working with ballpark estimates.

So, when the design is set and you know exactly what you're building, you're good to figure out the full budget. This budget will be submitted with your architectural drawings to the appraiser and must include a cost for every trade—even those tasks you plan to handle yourself.

We usually keep two versions of the budget: One for ourselves and one for the appraisal.

For example, if you plan to install the drywall yourself to save money, your version of the budget might list $0 for drywall labor. However, in the appraiser's copy, you should include a professional estimate for that work. Let's say you want to do the painting yourself—if you received a $7,000 quote from a painter, you would list $7,000 in the appraiser's budget but $0 in your copy.

This approach ensures the appraiser understands the full market value of the construction, while your personal budget reflects your actual savings. The goal is for the appraisal to be based on what it would cost *anyone* to build the project, not just what it costs *you* with your own labor.

> TIP: When putting together your budget, don't inflate the costs—ever. That's considered fraud. It might seem like a harmless way to make your numbers "fit," but if the bank has any doubts, they can (and often will) ask for written estimates from licensed contractors to verify the amounts you've listed. They're not just funding your project; they're evaluating the value of the build. If the numbers don't check out, you risk blowing the whole deal. Be honest, be realistic, and keep things clean—it's just not worth the shortcut.

REAL TALK: TWO BUDGETS, NO B.S.

Worried that keeping two versions of your budget might feel dishonest? Don't be. This is a completely legit and strategic move—as long as both versions are based on *real numbers*.

- Your **personal budget** reflects what you'll *actually spend*—especially if you're doing some of the work yourself or getting materials at a discount.

- The **appraiser's budget** shows what it would cost if you were to hire professionals for every single task—because that's how they calculate the market value of the build.

This isn't about inflating or faking numbers—it's about showing *value*. The appraiser needs to assess what the property is worth in a typical market scenario, not a DIY one. You need to track your actual expenses.

And here's the kicker: if you got hurt in Week 1 of the build and couldn't physically do the work yourself, you'd *have to* hire pros to finish the job. In that case, the appraiser's version of the budget becomes reality. It's a backup plan in disguise.

Two budgets. Two purposes. Both honest. Both essential.

BUDGET FLEXIBILITY AND CONTINGENCY

While it's okay to go slightly over budget when building your dream home, staying within the budget is essential when constructing an income property to ensure positive cash flow. Remember, you're not building for the sake of the fancy Instagram post, you're building whatever is cost effective and would make the numbers work for your investment goal.

Keeping that in mind, I find it's always best to set the budget higher than anticipated. Even with accurate expense tracking, there will always be unexpected expenses. Set aside a portion of funds to cover unexpected costs or emergencies that could arise during the course of the project (AKA: contingency budget) of *at least* five percent of the total project cost, or a minimum of $25,000, is a good starting point. For instance, if the total project cost is $600,000, your contingency could be at least $30,000. For smaller projects, like one costing $350,000, a $25,000 contingency may be more appropriate. If you feel safer increasing this amount and you have room in the budget, go for it. Some say planning for 10-15 percent of the budget is more accurate. In either case, it's there to provide you with a safety cushion that you hopefully won't have to use, but still crucial to plan for.

MAINTAINING A BUILD COST AND LOAN-TO-VALUE RATIO BELOW 80 PERCENT

Now, let's be clear: The ultimate goal is that your final mortgage will pay back all your construction costs + *extra*. You don't want your build costs to exceed the final pay out and have to leave money in the deal. You want to be able to pull out money so you can reinvest, like the BRRRR strategy I talked about in Chapter 6.

Perhaps you'd prefer to be funded at an even lower LTV ratio for reasons such as maintaining positive cash flow or for security to make sure you are not over leveraged. But even if your goal is to max out the loan and to take out as much money as possible, the problem still remains at keeping the cost to build as low as possible.

Though honestly, the only *sure* way that I've ever known in achieving this, are with the two words so many of you are dreading: Sweat equity. Or, DYI. Yep. Sorry guys, but it truly is our best trick yet.

> *"To get results no one else has, you have to do the work*
> *no one else is ready to do" - Autumn Calebrese.*

These days, we typically handle tasks such as design, drafting, project management, flooring, trim, kitchen installation, landscaping and all the little finishing touches at the end. And trust me, the finishing touches are usually endless. Thankfully, we now have two full time workers that help us with this so we are not alone anymore.

When we first started though, the list of things Rob and I did ourselves was so long that it would probably be shorter to list the things we didn't do. We would do everything I mentioned above, plus some interior framing, stair framing, insulation, drywall install (some projects Rob even did the mudding and sanding), painting, and in our early days, Rob would even do the electrical work himself.

Today though, we try to outsource more and more, but what we outsource can depend on the project's complexity, the budget, and the schedule. Ultimately, balancing your DIY efforts and outsourcing depends on your goals, available skills, and the financial numbers.

BUDGET EXAMPLE

To help guide you, I've included an example budget from one of our fourplex projects. Note that these are not exact numbers, but pretty darn close. And do not mistake our costs for what your costs would be. This example was chosen to demonstrate a more relatable project when we didn't have full-time labor. This build happened at the beginning of the Covid-19 pandemic when material and labor costs hadn't yet soared, and we were building two other fourplexes at the same time so there was a good balance between what we outsourced and what we DIY'd, making it relatable to most.

You'll notice the projected budget was higher than the actual cost—a result you'll want to aim for. This way, the projected budget can be fully financed, and any remaining funds from the actual cost can be kept while still maintaining a positive cash flow.

Budget Example found on our Website. Look for the 'Toolkit' download at www.thenewbuildcouple.com

12 STEPS FOR KEEPING BUILDING COSTS LOW

Building a multi-unit project is no small investment, but there are smart ways to keep costs down without cutting corners on quality or function. Here's how you can design efficiently, stay on top of your build, and make the most of the resources you already have.

1. INITIAL PLANNING: SETTING GOALS FOR SIMPLICITY AND COST-EFFECTIVENESS

The first step in keeping construction costs low is to have a clear and detailed discussion with your architect or designer. Clearly communicate your goals for simplicity and cost-effectiveness. Ensure the design is straightforward, avoiding wasted space, odd corners, bays, or angles. Expensive construction systems like ICF should also be avoided unless that's your preference. Instead, aim for standardized construction to keep things simple and manageable.

In Ontario, for example, the code allows you to choose from different "packages" for wall composition and R-value ratings based on your heating system. If you're opting for natural gas, you won't need as much R-value as with electric heating. Ask your designer to clarify the differences and suggest the most cost-effective solution before starting the design process. Today, Rob and I prefer electric heating with the extra insulation, but when we started we opted for natural gas. They both have their advantages and disadvantages, but basically we prefer to avoid having a 2nd utility company to deal with if we can. There's also less maintenance and danger going with an electric heat pump as opposed to Co2 leaks or whatnot with natural gas.

2. CONSULT WITH EXPERTS EARLY: HVAC AND INVESTOR INPUT

Heating and cooling systems (HVAC) are a complex thing because there are so many ways to go about it. It can be a big chunk of your budget. Consult with an HVAC specialist to ensure you're making the most informed choices. However, in our experience, it's even more beneficial to consult with other investor-builders who have gone through similar projects. Their input is often invaluable in making decisions on which systems will work best in your building.

Rob and I always take past experiences into consideration when working on the early designs. If you wait towards the end of the design to start thinking about HVAC, you risk messing up the floor plan. Rob visualizes the installation of plumbing, electrical, and HVAC systems from the start to minimize complications later. This way, we rework the design until it's cost-effective and easy to execute.

3. SIMPLE AND FUNCTIONAL FLOOR PLANS

A compact, functional, and straightforward floor plan is essential. It maximizes usable space and minimizes construction complexity. A simple layout naturally leads to a more straightforward roof design and reduces the need for complex engineering requirements.

Work closely with your draftsman to keep structural elements straightforward. A square building, with minimized joist spans and easy-to-build design elements, helps keep your budget on track. This allows the structural engineer to spend minimal time on the project, which reduces overall costs.

We were once designing a 6-plex on a lot with a steep hill covering about two-thirds of the back portion, and swampy soil at the base of the hill. To avoid costly soil prep and complex footings, we knew the building's footprint needed to be positioned toward the front of the lot, completely steering clear of that back hill. However, accounting for the required parking at the very front left us with a wide but not-so-deep buildable area.

As we started laying out the design, between the garage bays we wanted to include and the goal of giving each unit its own private entrance and staircase, the project was becoming more complicated and expensive to build, given the limited space we had to work with. After a couple of weeks of brainstorming and running into design roadblocks, I decided to completely redesign the project.

We removed the garage bays, combined the entrances into two shared staircases for all six units, and squared off the design—simplifying *everything*. This not only made the exterior more visually appealing, but it also created more spacious units. Everything flowed much better and became a more straightforward, efficient, and cost-effective build. It went from a project where we felt discouraged to build it, to a project we couldn't wait to start because we could easily envision the entire build process now. The transformation brought it to life.

4. SIMPLIFYING ROOF DESIGN

Another key strategy to reduce construction costs is to simplify the roof design. Avoid steep slopes and intricate design elements, which can increase labor and material costs, as well as the likelihood of on-site mistakes. A straightforward, low-pitch roof simplifies construction, reduces the need for specialized trusses, and minimizes future maintenance issues.

When your initial building footprint is simple, the roof design should follow naturally in its simplicity. In my earlier design days, clients often brought me pictures from Pinterest of beautiful houses they wanted to replicate. My first question was always, "What's your budget for this build?"—because many times, the roof design alone would push them over their budget. The problem is often in the roof: intricate designs look beautiful but are costly.

When building an investment property, it's crucial to balance aesthetics with practicality. Don't invest in a roof design that won't bring in additional rental income. It's all about optimizing costs where it matters most.

5. BE YOUR OWN GENERAL CONTRACTOR (OR HIRE A PM INSTEAD)

Acting as your own general contractor (GC) can save you 10–15 percent in management fees—on a $600,000 build, that's up to $90,000. While it's a challenging role, it gets easier with every project. One smart way to ease into it is by shadowing an experienced GC. Offer to compensate them for their time—it's an investment that could save you thousands by helping you avoid rookie mistakes.

If you're not quite ready to take on the GC role yourself, consider hiring a project manager (PM) at a fixed rate instead. For example, if a GC might cost $90,000 on your build, budgeting $40,000 for a PM could give you hands-on guidance without losing full control of the project—and still save you $50K. That's a win-win.

6. LEVERAGE SWEAT EQUITY

Sweat equity—putting in your own labor—is one of the most powerful tools in your toolkit. Even taking on smaller tasks like painting, landscaping, or site cleanup can make a meaningful dent in your budget. Not only does it save money, but it also keeps you closely involved, ensuring everything is done to your standards.

That said, if you've hired a GC, you may not be allowed to participate in the work due to liability and insurance constraints. Most GCs won't let you get involved unless there's a special arrangement. If you're working under your own liability and insurance (with or without a hired PM), then sweat equity becomes a viable—and often essential—strategy.

For us, it was everything. Rob and I did nearly everything ourselves in our first five years: design, framing, painting, trim, kitchens—you name it. It's how we kept 100 percent of the profits and equity on all our builds. That sweat equity gave us the cash flow to scale—whether that meant making competitive cash offers on land or hiring more trades to grow faster. We built our wealth with our hands first, so we could later build it with our team.

7. STANDARDIZE MATERIALS AND COLORS

Choosing standard sizes and materials helps reduce waste, streamline construction, and cut costs. Custom options, while appealing, often come with higher prices and delays. For instance, white windows and light-colored fascia and eavestroughs are usually more affordable than custom colors. We usually do a more custom design with black windows only at the front of the building and white windows with simple palettes on the sides and at the back. We also stick to locally available, standardized materials to simplify ordering and installation, driving even more savings.

8. BULK PURCHASING

Buying materials in bulk allows you to take advantage of volume discounts. Work with suppliers to secure the best prices on large orders. Not only does this reduce costs, but it also ensures you have a steady supply of materials, minimizing delays.

However, be cautious about ordering too far in advance. A friend of mine once ordered all the windows for his building because a store offered a promotion, but he was still waiting on the city's permit approval. Turned out, the city required triple-pane windows due to the heating-design package he planned to use, which wasn't what he had ordered. Fortunately, he was able to adjust by changing his heating package and purchasing the right equipment to compensate.

9. EFFICIENT PLANNING AND EXECUTION

Plan your project thoroughly to avoid changes and rework. Clear, detailed plans help prevent misunderstandings and ensure that everyone is on the same page. Efficient planning reduces the likelihood of costly delays and modifications during the construction phase. Discuss the systems and the finishes with your trades ahead of time so everyone is on the same page of what the finished outcome is supposed to be. If you make changes to the drawings, you absolutely need to think of every trade this change could affect, and then ensure they all get the new drawings and new scope to avoid expensive mix ups.

10. HIRE SKILLED LABOR WISELY

While hiring the cheapest labor might seem like a cost-saving strategy, investing in skilled workers can save money in the long run. Skilled laborers work faster, with higher quality, reducing the need for rework and ensuring the project stays on schedule.

If, for example, you hire a drywall installer who's cheap but unreliable, it could end up costing you more in delays and additional labor time to fix his work. The Mudder, for instance, may charge you extra if they have to spend hours cleaning up after the installer and fixing his crooked installation with additional mud and time. Or, if a plumber is cheaper than another, but you spend the first three years post-build dealing with plumbing-related maintenance calls or, worse, floods due to improper installation, you're not ahead. Always check references.

11. BALANCE COST-CUTTING WITH VALUE-BUILDING

While keeping costs low is important, it's just as crucial to invest in features that will actually make your property more desirable and profitable over time. Most tenants aren't won over by what kind of insulation you used or whether your HVAC system is the latest model. What they *do* care about is the layout, the finishings, the natural light, how many bathrooms there are, whether there's a balcony or backyard, and whether the unit feels like somewhere they can actually enjoy living.

This is where smart design choices make a huge difference. Open-concept living areas, modern kitchens, ensuite bathrooms, private outdoor space, and in-unit laundry go a lot further in attracting great tenants than energy efficiency alone. Those features help justify higher rents and lower turnover.

That said, some behind-the-scenes investments still matter—like proper soundproofing, durable materials that reduce long-term maintenance, and decent windows that help with temperature control. The goal is to focus on *perceived value* while still protecting your bottom line. You want tenants to walk in and say, "This place feels worth the rent"—because that's where profitability begins.

12. THE KEEP IT SIMPLE, STUPID (KISS) PRINCIPLE

The "Keep It Simple, Stupid" (KISS) principle is invaluable in construction. Simple designs are easier to build, require fewer specialized skills, and often result in a more efficient process. By embracing simplicity in every aspect—from layout to material choices—you can reduce costs associated with labor, materials, and potential errors.

If you implement these strategies, managing construction costs will be much easier, while ensuring your project is built to high standards and offers long-term value. Focus on simplicity, efficiency, and thoughtful planning to maximize your investment and achieve a successful build.

When in doubt, remember: Keep it simple!

DISCOUNT TRICKS

There are many ways to get discounts during a build. You can search on Google or Instagram and find great ideas from people craftier than me. Some of our simple ideas include the following:

- Visiting a local lumberyard and introducing yourself to the estimators or manager. Explain your project and inquire if they have programs or discount rates for contractor accounts or a minimum-volume project. This may result in discounts of 5–10 percent, maybe even 15 percent, off the retail price.

- Shopping at big box stores like Home Depot and taking advantage of sales and contractor member benefits, such as 18 months of interest-free purchases when signing up for one of their credit cards.

- Checking Facebook Marketplace or online stores like Wayfair for discounted items like vanities, electrical fixtures, bathtubs, appliances, and mirrors.

- Shopping during the big sale events of course, like Black Friday / Cyber Monday. I usually score big at that time of year for my builds.

- Taking advantage of new construction tax rebates by consulting with a qualified accountant who has experience in these types of accounts. In Canada, the tax rebate process for investment properties differs completely from an owner occupied, single-family home and can be very complex. Therefore, investing in an experienced accountant who can maneuver through the process can result in significant savings.

Shopping the Trades

If you're looking for reliable tradespeople for your first build, start by reaching out to local lumberyards, architects, designers, or even your realtor. Word of mouth from other builders and investors can also be helpful. But keep in mind that trade recommendations are often highly valued and not easily shared, because some don't want to lose the great service they have from their trade by sharing them with everyone.

To approach this, start by making sure you're in the bidding phase and serious about your project. If you don't have a prior relationship with the person you're asking, offer something in exchange to show appreciation. We always thank those who recommend good trades to us, as we value our relationships.

Another approach is to start with one trade, such as a civil engineer recommended by the municipality, who can then refer you to other specialists like an excavation crew or a foundation contractor. Those trades can then refer you to a plumber and a framer, and so on.

During the bidding phase, we typically limit our requests to two or three quotes max. per trade type to respect others' time. Avoid asking too many trades for quotes without clear intent, as this can hurt your reputation in the close-knit construction community. Building loyal relationships with your hired trades will serve you better in the long run.

This trade list is also found in our website's Toolkit download.

TIP: It's also best that you ask for quotes only after the construction drawings are completed. Requesting quotes with preliminary designs can be a waste of time for tradespeople, and many will either ignore the request or overbid to protect themselves for three reasons:

1) there's usually too much missing information on the plans.

2) they'll think you're not serious yet.

3) they'll be afraid they will have to prepare multiple estimates as your design may still change. While it's understandable that you may want an estimate of costs before proceeding with the full drawings, this is the proper sequence of the process when doing it correctly and if you want to be taken seriously.

DON'T FORGET THE "SOFT COSTS"

Soft costs, also known as indirect costs, are essential expenses not directly tied to physical construction but crucial to the development process. They can add up fast and affect your overall budget, so it's important to plan for them carefully to avoid any surprises down the road.

- One major soft cost is **Land Transfer Tax**, called Property Transfer Tax or Real Estate Transfer Tax in other regions. This tax is charged on property purchases and varies by location and property value, so including it in your budget is crucial to avoid surprises.

- **Engineering fees** are another critical soft cost, covering services from structural, civil, and mechanical engineers. These professionals conduct site assessments, produce designs, and consult on technical requirements to ensure project safety and functionality. Anticipate these expenses based on your project's size and municipal requirements.

- **Design fees** cover the costs of architects and draftsmen who develop the construction drawings and design specs. This phase establishes the project's foundation, impacting functionality, aesthetics, and code compliance.

- **Permits and approvals** from local authorities are also required to meet zoning, building code, and safety standards. These fees vary by project size and location, so budgeting for them—and potential approval delays—helps keep your project timeline on track.

- **Financing fees** include loan origination costs, interest during construction, and other lender-related expenses. Work with your financial advisor to ensure these charges are accurately reflected in your project budget.

- For larger developments, **feasibility studies** may also be required, particularly if financing exceeds certain limits (e.g., $2 million). These studies assess market viability, environmental impact, and infrastructure needs, helping identify potential challenges early.

- Other soft costs include **legal fees, project management, and insurance**. Legal fees cover contracts and agreements, while project management fees apply if you hire professionals to oversee the project. Builder's Risk insurance, essential in Ontario for new builds, provides coverage against construction-related risks.

- Lastly, the **contingency fund** is also part of the soft costs.

Consulting local professionals, such as builders, CPAs, and realtors, can help you uncover hidden soft costs specific to your market. You should include a dedicated budget section for these expenses.

TRACKING THE BUDGET

Effective expense tracking is essential during any construction project. To maintain smooth operations, it's best to set up a reliable system before the project begins. While there are many advanced software options, you can choose to keep it simple with an Excel sheet. This is how we operated for years. Our sheet had two main columns: "Projected Budget" and "Actual Costs." Each time we received an invoice, we updated the sheet, downloaded the invoice, renamed it with the job number and payment date, and filed it electronically. We also saved electronic copies of all in-store purchase receipts. At the end of each month, our virtual assistant organizes these folders, updates the budgets, and does basic bookkeeping.

Today, we use accounting software. The previously stated invoice procedure still remains, but the software is connected to our bank accounts in order to minimize the error gap. At the end of every quarter, we transfer all records to our accountant, who then completes the reporting to the Canada Revenue Agency.

If you're working without a bookkeeper, try to track expenses monthly. For a low-tech approach, keep a notebook and physical folder for receipts in your vehicle to stay organized while on the go. Alternatively, a mobile expense tracking app can make it easy to upload invoices and receipts directly to your computer. This is an efficient way to track expenses, flag issues early, and keep your project on course.

TOP THREE TAKEAWAYS:

1. **Budget Planning Requires Specifics**: You can't accurately plan your construction budget until you've secured financing, chosen your land, and finalized the design. The budget should include all expenses, even those tasks you plan to do yourself. A version for the appraiser should include professional estimates, while your personal version can reflect actual savings from DIY work and discounted items.

2. **Contingency and Flexibility Are Key**: Construction projects often come with unexpected expenses, so it's crucial to set aside a contingency budget (at least five percent of total costs). While it's okay to go over budget slightly, keeping costs under control is essential for maintaining positive cash flow in income properties.

3. **Don't Underestimate Soft Costs:** While hard costs like materials and labor often steal the spotlight, soft costs can significantly impact your budget. Ensure you account for essential expenses like land transfer taxes, engineering fees, design fees, permits, financing charges, and legal fees. Planning for these will help you avoid financial surprises and keep your project on track.

CHAPTER 12

THE PERMIT PROCESS

Now the planning phase is done, the budget has been prepared, and the financing is in place, you're almost ready to apply for the building permit. However, there are still some steps to take to complete your application, and sometimes the process can seem a bit daunting. As I mentioned before, you'll need to contact the municipality you are building in and ask them to provide you with a list of what you'll need for your specific project.

Here's the typical list of documents you need to include for a building permit application:

1. You need a **survey plan** of the lot. A land survey is a drawing made by professional land surveyors that determines a property's boundaries. It's the map of your lot. You can request one from the seller during your offer to purchase, but if the seller doesn't have a survey plan, you'll likely need to hire a land surveyor to have one drawn up. Sometimes the municipality will keep a copy in their archives, or you can call a surveyor to see if they have it, and pay them a fee to retrieve it. Your real estate agent may also be able to find one in their database. However, an up to date survey may still be required as sometimes the surveys on file are quite dated.

2. You need the **construction plans** for your project that have been drawn by your draftsman. They should include all elevations (front, back, and side views), floor plans, construction details, notes, and a site plan. Some construction plans may

also include the mechanical plans if such are required, (e.g., electrical, HVAC, and plumbing), but often you'll need those drawn by others (e.g. mechanical engineers).

FRONT ELEVATION

3. You may also need a stamp from a **structural engineer** to review all structural components such as the beams and posts sizes, footings and pad sizes, truss designs, floor joist designs, etc.

4. Our municipality also requires the **floor joist layout and roof truss layout**. The truss manufacturer does these, and our lumber supplier takes care of requesting them from the manufacturer while they work on our material estimate.

5. You'll likely need a civil engineer for a **grading plan**, which prepares the lot for development and outlines the elevations, slopes, drainage patterns, and swale locations. Here's an example proposal of such for a triplex project we did in 2023. It includes everything you would need for a small project that has municipal water and sewers, from start to finish.

> 1. **Limited Topographical Survey with GPS – $1250.00+HST**
>   a. Required to prepare grading and servicing plan
> 2. **Site grading, drainage and Servicing plan – $2,850.00+HST**
>   a. Required for permit application
> 3. **Founding Soil Inspection - $325.00+HST**
>   a. Required at excavation
> 4. **As-built plan - $850.00+HST**
>   a. To be carried out 2024 – required to release deposit from City

6. If you need a septic field, check if the civil engineer can also do a **septic design**. Some do, and some don't. If not, you'll need to find a septic designer. Note that usually it's best to get the septic design completed *before* you get the grading plan done. These two usually work hand in hand.

7. Some municipalities may even request a copy of the **budget** and/or some quotes for the project with the application. (This is something I've seen.)

8. You'll need to fill out the municipality's **application forms** and provide proof that you own the property, such as your deed to the land.

9. Finally, you'll need to pay the permit fees.

Once you've gathered all your documents, you're finally ready to apply for the permit! The fees may be collected upfront when you submit the application, or only when the permit is approved and ready to be picked up. As long as you keep in mind that fees can vary significantly from one place to another.

In Ontario, generally DCs are very high. But hopefully you can take advantage of Bill 23 and certain rebates offered through that. And if you bought an infill property where you demolish to rebuild, you should get a development fee credit for the house you demolished. Even for a small single-family home or a cottage, the cost will start at $30,000. And on top of that, our city announced that the rates are going to increase by 85 percent in the next year. That's almost doubling! In comparison, we once applied to build a cottage in the neighboring province of Quebec that only cost us $200. Evidently, it's not the same across the board. Make sure you have a good idea of the cost of your permit ahead of time so you can budget properly.

A NOTE ON LARGER DEVELOPMENTS

With bigger projects come bigger responsibilities. The permit process isn't any smaller for large developments. There is always more paperwork to submit, more studies to do, and more money to spend before getting the permit.

For example, the project I mentioned in an earlier chapter where we started with a sixplex but the goal is to eventually develop a total of

48 units into two lots. The first 24 units would be owned by us and the second 24 by a friend. The goal was to split on certain costs among both sites. As I mentioned previously, we initially had the pre-consultation, and then the zoning change that we split. Now, the next step will be the site plan control application. This will include a topographical survey, floor plans, elevations and a 3D image, as well as specific studies such as a noise study and a traffic study — which can cost around $10,000. Afterward, we'll move on to septic designs, which may include certain types of environmental studies, and possibly more. Then finally, we should be able to finalize all the drawings and officially apply for the permit.

By the time we're ready to apply for the permit, we may end up spending a total of $50,000. Plus, the permit and development fees can be about $250,000 per site. Or, 460k per site if the city goes through with the 85 percent increase. We split up this project in multiple phases, and depending on how things go, we may only complete the final phase several years from now.

For now, we built only a sixplex for Phase 1 because it didn't need to go through the site plan control application with the city, and because we wanted to take advantage of Bill 23 and save on the development charges. Instead of paying $92k in DCs, we paid about $53k. That way we could at least monetize the land. Although we fought hard for that credit. If any of you have been following us on Instagram, I posted about going in front of City council and winning a case on DCs and how the province left a lot of ambiguity in that legislation. Well that was for this project. We had to consult with lawyers and base our case on recent precedents the city had set, and finally the council voted in favor of giving us the $39k credit (4 votes in favor, 3 against).

We purchased the land in 2020, but didn't break ground on Phase 1 until the fall of 2024—only because we reduced it from a nine unit, to a six. If we hadn't made that change, who knows when we would have been able to start. This is why these types of projects are not recommended for beginners unless you have strategic partners with enough capital and experience to lead the process and maybe front the costs until traditional financing comes into play.

TOP THREE TAKEAWAYS:

1. **Thorough Preparation is Key:** Before applying for a building permit, it's crucial to gather all necessary documents, including a survey plan, construction plans, and potentially a grading plan or septic design. Each municipality may have specific requirements, so it's important to contact them early and prepare accordingly.

2. **The Permit Process Can Be Costly and Time-Consuming:** Permit fees and associated costs, such as development charges, can vary significantly depending on the municipality and the scope of the project. It's essential to budget for these expenses in advance to avoid financial surprises. Larger developments, in particular, may require extensive studies and substantial fees before even beginning construction.

3. **Complex Projects Require More Resources and Time:** For larger developments, the permit process is more intricate and requires additional paperwork, studies, and potentially higher fees. These projects are not recommended for beginners unless they have experienced partners to guide them through the process and help cover upfront costs. Strategic planning and phased development can help manage these complexities.

CHAPTER 13

BUILDING TIPS

THE BUILD PROCESS

Every building project is unique. At times, the process can seem overwhelming and complex. If this is your first-time building, you may be nervous about the proper order to take. I remember feeling nervous about that too. We would worry about getting called out for being a bad builder or not passing inspections and making a mess of things. But remember a few things: First of all, the trades know. Maybe not always the front line workers on site, but the owners of the companies or the crew lead usually know the proper order of things. When you're calling them to line up the work, if you're unsure about the right sequence of something, ask them what they think. They should be glad to offer assistance and show off their expertise.

When you pick up your permit, most municipalities will include a list of inspections that will follow in their respective order. This can be a good guide to follow, but below I'm giving you an oversimplified step-by-step list of *our* typical building process. Hopefully this gives you a good idea and makes it easier for you to understand the general process. Remember though, the process may vary significantly depending on your location:

1. Clear the site of vegetation, debris, trees, and large rocks;

2. Level or dig the site and prepare for footings and utilities;

3. at this stage, we get our building permit and inspection for underside of footings;

4. Pour foundation walls and waterproof the foundation;

5. Backfill the foundation and pass inspection;

6. Prepare underground plumbing and pass inspection;

7. Frame the building and pass inspection;

8. Install roofing;

9. Install the HVAC system, plumbing, and electrical wiring and pass inspection for each;

10. Begin the exterior finishes;

11. Complete insulation of walls and ceilings and pass inspection;

12. Install drywall, flooring, and kitchens;

13. Complete final electrical, HVAC, and plumbing work;

14. Finalize the interior and exterior details;

15. Pass occupancy inspections (interior and exterior);

16. Landscape and pass the grading inspection.

Like I've said before, if you still feel unsure or nervous about the process, consider shadowing another contractor to learn. Or, see if you can arrange with a contractor to pay them or exchange services if there's anything you can offer, for them simply taking your phone calls when you have questions about the process.

Try not to get stuck in "analysis paralysis," which is when you over analyse a strategy to a point where you don't actually do anything. Remember that another great way to learn a process is to throw yourself in it and learn on the fly, obviously while taking calculated risks. But to help you further, I've compiled eight essential tips in the next section to help streamline your project.

NINE ESSENTIAL TIPS

These tips will not only make your projects hassle-free, they'll also make management during tenancy easier. Remember to adapt them as needed for your specific region.

TIP #1: INSURANCE POLICIES

Once you're ready to break ground, ensure you have the appropriate construction insurance coverage, known here as a builder's risk policy. This type of policy typically covers risks like fire, theft, vandalism, and weather-related damage during the construction phase, protecting the owner, contractor, or developer from financial loss. Builder's risk policies usually remain active until the building is completed and occupied. However, these policies don't cover injuries or damage to third parties, so it's wise to also carry contractor general liability (CGL) insurance especially if you're acting as the GC.

Obviously, these terms may vary from one location to the next, but basically you need to make sure you're covered for fire, theft, vandalism, and liability for injuries and damage to third parties. Consult with your insurance broker early on to understand coverage needs and budget for this essential cost. It may also be a good idea to verify with the financial institution that would be financing your build to see if they have any specific coverage needs in their conditions. They usually ask to be added on a specific policy as a mortgagee and ask for a copy of that upon first disbursement.

TIP #2: FOUNDATION AND FRAMING

Securing experienced foundation and framing contractors is crucial, since they establish the structure and stability of your building. These trades set the framework for compliance with safety codes and standards, helping avoid costly mistakes down the line. A quality framer ensures walls are straight and aligned, which impacts everything from floor leveling to the proper installation of finishes. For instance, framing walls without precision can cause issues such as uneven floors, misaligned trusses, or shifting walls, all of which affect both the durability and appearance of your units. To make sure you're hiring reliable professionals, ask for recommendations, pictures of previous work and verify references. When calling references, ask them to rate the quality of the work on a scale of one to ten, how quick the trade was to complete the work and if they would hire them again.

TIP #3: MECHANICAL SYSTEMS

Efficient mechanical systems are fundamental to multi-unit buildings and directly impact tenant comfort and operational costs. Key components include:

- **Plumbing:** Plumbing is one of those behind-the-walls systems that you can't cut corners on—it needs to be done right from the start. This includes everything from getting clean water into the house, getting wastewater out, and in some cases, tying into or installing a septic system if you're building in a rural area. And it's one trade we will not do ourselves. We prefer to have a professional behind that along with their warranty. Working with water is always tricky, if something leaks and creates water damage, I want to pass on that headache as much as possible.

  When it comes to hot water tanks, we've found it's more cost-effective to purchase them rather than rent. Rental programs might seem convenient, but those monthly fees add up over time and chip away at your cash flow. Owning them outright means one less ongoing cost to worry about.

  That said, if a rental tank fails and floods your unit (which *has* happened to us), the rental company will typically handle the replacement or repair, no questions asked. From there, you can go through your own insurance, and they'll take care of pursuing the rental company if needed. It's not a seamless process, but it can take some of the pressure off in a crisis. Again, it's all about deciding where you want to save money—and where you want peace of mind.

  In some basement units, we've installed radiant in-floor heating before, and tankless systems were a great space-saver for those. They also help streamline your mechanical room layout, which is useful in smaller units. That said, we've noticed tenants will love the warmth and comfort of the in-floor heat, but often prefer traditional hot water tanks because they tend to deliver hot water more quickly, especially when multiple fixtures are being used at once. So it's always a balance between efficiency, cost, available space and tenant satisfaction.

> TIP: When possible, ask your draftsman to place all your rooms with plumbing fixtures in one cluster. For example, in our 6 plex, we placed bathrooms directly behind kitchens towards the middle wall, which was mirrored in the unit next to it. So all the plumbing was centralized in the building. This helps save on the installation process and just makes everything more efficient.

- **Electrical:** Electrical is one of those systems where clean planning upfront makes everything easier down the road. We give each unit its own 100-amp panel and a separate hydro meter. It's a bit more work during construction, but totally worth it—there's no need to split utility bills or track usage manually. It simplifies tenant management and keeps everyone accountable for their own usage.

  We also make sure there are plenty of outlets, and that breaker panels are easily accessible but secure. It's one of those little things that makes a big difference for both trades and tenants. But we try to be strategic when we position them. We find a place near the meter but also near the kitchen which is where the bulk of the wiring is to make the wiring as efficient as possible. The Hydro company here also requires that the meter be placed near the driveway or parking for easy access especially during winter.

  If you're considering adding EV chargers down the line or using electric baseboard heaters in any units, it's a good idea to talk to your electrician early in the design phase to make sure your service size can handle it. Upgrading later can be expensive.

- **HVAC (Heating, Ventilation, and Air Conditioning):** The HVAC system is often the most complex and critical of the mechanical systems, given the variety of options available and its significant impact on monthly utility costs. Choosing the right setup is essential for both efficiency and cost savings.

Over the years, we've experimented with different HVAC configurations; in fact, most of our buildings have distinct setups based on evolving technology and cost considerations.

In Ontario, natural gas heating has traditionally been more economical than electric options. For a while, we installed high-efficiency natural gas furnaces paired with central AC in top units. Then some basement units had high efficiency gas fireplaces and we added electric baseboard heaters as supplemental heat, while other units had in-floor radiant heat instead.

However, electric heat pumps have recently gained popularity due to their efficiency and compact design, eliminating the need for large mechanical rooms and certified gas installers. Heat pumps are also environmentally friendly, easy to install, and double as air conditioning units, making them a versatile choice.

For recent projects, we've standardized on electric heat pumps as the primary heating source, and electric baseboards in each room as a secondary heat source. We plan for heat pumps in the initial design, positioning them centrally within the unit but near an exterior wall for efficiency and ease of installation. Additionally, it's worthwhile to check for local grants, which can help offset the costs of high-efficiency products.

This goes without saying, but even if you plan to DIY one of these systems, consult professionals and get proper permits to ensure the systems are safe, efficient, and up to code.

TIP #4: FLOORING

Careful flooring selection affects maintenance needs and tenant satisfaction, especially in high-traffic areas. While ceramic tile is resilient, we avoid it because it's colder underfoot, has poor sound absorption, and requires frequent grout cleaning. It's also a bigger job to change out later if needed. We avoid carpet due to hygiene concerns and non-durability.

Our preferred flooring is the luxury vinyl plank (LVP). We opt for it due to its durability, scratch and water-resistance, its warmth on the feet and the fact that since it's not a wood product like laminate, it won't promote mold growth when in contact with water or humidity. A lesson learned however: Pairing cheap LVP with foam underlay can lead to cracking and separation, so we now choose thicker planks with integrated underlay for longevity. Avoiding maintenance calls on damaged flooring is worth the upfront cost.

That being said, we still struggle to find an easy-to-install plank system that doesn't separate with temperature changes. One successful installation is a floating system where the perimeter is glued on, but it's messier and lengthier to install. Or, one that is fully glued on. Which is exactly what we've installed in our last 3 builds. So far so good in terms of maintenance. As long as we don't need to deal with maintenance calls on separated planks from the clip-on systems, we're happy landlords.

TIP #5: EXTERIOR FINISHES

Exterior finishes are always a balance between durability, visual appeal, and cost savings. In our area, vinyl siding is common because it's cost-effective and comes in a wide range of customizable options. In our last couple of builds, we've mixed materials—using aluminum siding and higher-end vertical vinyl at the front, along with some stonework for added texture and curb appeal.

The triplex below is one of my favourite models. The brick was a lucky find from a liquidation sale at our local lumber yard. We used high-quality vertical black vinyl siding, paired it with brown aluminum accents, black windows, and a black garage door. The remaining sides of the building were finished in standard horizontal vinyl and white windows.

Even though the building has a fairly basic, square footprint—and the front elevation was originally quite flat and plain—we were able to elevate the look significantly. By mixing materials and playing with contrast and texture, it ended up being one of our best-looking builds.

For the roof, we use high-quality, lifetime composite shingles for their durability compared to standard builder-grade shingles. While metal roofs or wood siding are attractive, they don't increase building value in our region and add unnecessary expense. Choose finishes based on your area's climate and that doesn't break the bank, and aim for options that are both attractive and low-maintenance.

TIP #6: INTERIOR FINISHES

The choice of interior finishes for a rental property is along the same lines as that for exterior finishes. They should be durable, low-maintenance, and appealing. Finding a balance can be tricky, and the result isn't always easy or perfect. Here's what we typically use:

1. **Flooring**: LVP, for the reasons stated previously.

2. **Kitchen cabinets**: We find Ikea cabinets offer both quality and flexibility at a lower price than custom cabinetry. The cabinet doors can be easily swapped out if damaged, making updates simpler. They are easy to assemble and install and they continue to improve their systems every year. Our in-house guys can easily assemble all the cabinets in just a few hours.

The downside: It can be a pain to learn their online planning tool and make sure you have all the pieces. It might be trial and error until you get it right. Our kitchen designs are almost identical in each unit so it has become very easy for us to complete our kitchen orders. Still, often they don't have everything in stock and it becomes a pain to track everything.

3. **Countertops**: Laminate countertops are cost-effective, easy to clean, and replaceable. We work with a local supplier for quick turnaround and have standardized our designs to streamline ordering and installation. We've used the Ikea countertops before but we prefer to use a local company. We send them a sketch of our measurements once the cabinets are installed and order the same style and profile each time. Yes, it may be adding extra steps to the entire kitchen installation process, rather than ordering from a cabinetry company that designs and installs from A-Z, but the money we save is substantial.

And no, we don't put in quartz or granite countertops because for one, the difference in price between those and laminate is always crazy. Second, tenants never really seem to notice nor care. The laminate we choose is a white with grey veins that mimics a quartz look.

4. **Neutral colors**: We stick to neutral tones like beige or gray, which appeal to a wide range of renters and are easy to repaint. Our current favorite shade is "Dried Mushroom" by Sico Paint.

5. **Good lighting**: We make sure the rental property has good lighting, including LED bulbs, and a combination of overhead and task lighting. We usually buy affordable, stylish, but simple fixtures that can be bought off the shelf at big box stores or on Amazon. I've often had tenants swap out fixtures to match their own style, taste, or need, and store the ones we had installed for several years. So, there's no point in putting up uber fancy or expensive fixtures.

6. **Appliances**: I know it's not the norm, and most of you won't agree with me on this, but we try to rent our units without any appliances. I'm talking fridge, stove, dishwasher, washer, and

dryer. We allow our tenants to provide their own appliances, as this approach reduces our maintenance calls by about 50 percent. The appliances that use water are the biggest pains, like the dishwasher and washer. Plus, I've heard stories about tenants stealing the appliances overnight and leaving. But the reality is that most tenants often don't know or care to properly maintain appliances, which has led to recurring issues.

For example, tenants calling saying their dryer no longer dried the clothes properly when all they needed to do was empty the lint drawer. Or, dishwashers malfunctioning because residents don't rinse dishes properly or neglect rinse aid, and other similar problems. By letting tenants bring their own appliances, we avoid the constant maintenance and replacement costs.

To achieve this, sometimes we need to offer the rents slightly lower than the market average, typically around $50–$75 less per unit. But it's absolutely worth it for us. If we absolutely must supply appliances to rent a unit, we try to limit it only to a fridge and stove, as these are the lowest-maintenance options. Plus, they are the bigger pieces which saves our walls from multiple dents during turnovers. We're transparent with potential tenants about our decision not to include other appliances, and encourage them to check local or online marketplaces, like Facebook Marketplace or Kijiji, where they can often find good deals on used appliances.

We didn't have any problems renting our units without appliances for almost 10 years. We had even started a wide trend among local landlords. Everyone was doing it. Which was great as it was almost becoming the norm in our area. Now recently, the market shifted and we're noticing more competition pop up. Therefore in order to continue finding great renters, we started supplying the fridge and stove while maintaining that $50-$75 below market value. The lower price hooks them in, and then they shop the used appliances online and notice it's doable. All the while we continue to reduce maintenance calls significantly.

7. **Affordable upgrades**: You could consider adding affordable upgrades like crown molding or wainscotting in less desirable units such as basement units. They will help enhance the overall look, feel, and appeal of the unit. We did wainscotting in a few of our basement units out of ripped MDF sheets. See image below. Just don't forget to consider the extra time it will take and cost you and weigh the pros and cons for if it's worth it or not.

TIP #7: HUMIDITY CONTROL

A simple adjustment to consider is to wire the exhaust fan in the bathrooms to the light switches.

That way, it's always running when the light is on, and tenants can't forget to turn on the fan during long hot showers. That protects the home from accumulative humidity and avoids mold. It's all about protecting your investment!

TIP #8: FLOOD CONTROL

Have you ever dealt with flooding in a rental unit? We have — more times than we can count. I'd guess at least a dozen... probably more. Honestly, we've experienced some form of water damage or flooding in nearly every building we own — some more than once.

We've seen it all. Here are just a few examples:

- A tenant flushing a towel down the toilet (yes, really)

- A build up of "flushable" wipes clogging the sewage pump in basement units with private septics - this is the most common one

- A fridge water line randomly malfunctioning

- A shower base leak

- Heat pump/AC condensation lines clogging, and overflowing

- Faulty or aging washing machine hoses

- Major condensation from high humidity

- And the worst of all: a spring storm that brought heavy snowmelt, followed by a power outage — which flooded four units at once and caused tens of thousands of dollars in damage.

This list could go on. If you haven't dealt with water damage yet, you will eventually. Every landlord I know has had some run-in with it—because when you own enough properties, it's only a matter of time. At this point, I honestly think we've faced just about every water-related crisis imaginable.

Some things are out of your control—it just comes with the territory. And here's the thing: building new doesn't make you immune. Sure, we might avoid some of the quirks that come with older, crooked houses, but water is the great equalizer. It finds its way in, whether your building is 50 years old or five weeks old. And when it does, it's always a pain to deal with.

What all these headaches have taught us is this: while you can't control everything, you *can* lower your risk through smart planning and preventative measures during the build phase. Here's how we now approach the scenarios I listed above:

Problem: A tenant flushed a towel down the toilet & A build up of "flushable" wipes clogging the sewage pump in basement units on private septics

Solution: Our leases now include a clear clause that states: *"Tenants must never flush ANYTHING other than toilet paper — not even flushable wipes... Tenants will be held responsible for any resulting damage."* This is especially critical in units on septic systems. I also make a point of verbally emphasizing it during key handoff with new tenants—because it's one of those small things that becomes a very expensive lesson if overlooked.

And yes, I hold tenants responsible when necessary. In most cases, the issue is caught quickly (usually right after flushing), so the tenant is only responsible for the plumber's service call and a bit of cleanup.

We also added another layer of protection after a costly mistake: our VA, Danick, now has it in his SOP to verify that all tenants maintain active insurance policies with proper liability coverage—and he checks this annually. Why? Because one tenant didn't renew their insurance, then caused significant flooding by flushing a towel. Since there was no coverage in place, our insurance took the full hit. Lesson learned. Now, tenant insurance is mandatory, and our management software helps us track and follow up on it each year.

Problem: Fridge water line malfunction

Solution: We no longer install fridge water lines. Tenants can use a filtered water dispenser or pitcher. One less potential leak to worry about.

Problem: Shower base leak

Solution: Invest in high-quality shower kits and surrounds, and hire skilled, licensed plumbers. Every detail needs to be sealed and triple-checked during install. Cutting corners here costs way more down the line.

Problems: Heat pump/AC condensation lines clogging, and overflowing & Faulty or aging washing machine hoses

Solution: Not much to be done here other than routine maintenance and yearly inspections. Just one of those things that might happen. As long as the leaks are reported to us promptly, we can send someone to fix it ASAP and avoid further damages. The lease clearly states that any leak or damage to the home must be reported within 3 days.

Problem: Excessive condensation from humidity

Solution: Make sure every unit has adequate ventilation and dehumidification. We now install heat pump/AC combos in all units — not just for comfort, but because they can help manage humidity. Most models have a dedicated dehumidifier setting.

Problem: Massive flooding from spring thaw + power outage

Solution: This one changed how we build entirely. We now install water-powered backup sump pumps in any property with a sump pit. These run on municipal water pressure, so they keep working during power outages — no electricity or battery needed. On our most recent sixplex, we went even further: because the building is on a private septic field, we installed a GenerLink* transfer switch connected to the basement units' panels. If the power goes out, tenants are informed to notify us, we will send someone to bring a portable generator and tenants can simply flip the GenerLink switch to run critical systems like sewage pumps. This way, the whole septic setup remains functional, and avoids sewer back ups — even in a storm.

NOTE: A **GenerLink** is a transfer switch device that's installed right at your home's hydro meter. It allows you to safely connect a portable generator to your home's electrical panel without any complicated wiring or need for extension cords running through windows or doors.

When the power goes out, you simply plug your generator into the GenerLink. It automatically disconnects your home from the grid to prevent backfeeding (which is dangerous for utility workers), and powers your home's essential circuits through the generator. You get to choose which circuits are powered — like your sump pump, fridge, or lights — depending on the generator's capacity.

In Ontario, GenerLink is approved by many local utilities and is especially popular in rural areas or properties with private septic systems, where keeping pumps running during outages is critical.

Water damage is no joke. It's costly, stressful, and always happens at the worst possible time. But remember that every bad experience is an opportunity to ask yourself "what process or procedure can I implement now to avoid or manage this situation better in the future?". When something happens, don't panic. Analyze, find a solution, then find a prevention.

TIP #9: DIY VS. DELEGATE – FINDING THE RIGHT MIX

DIYing in construction can definitely be a double-edged sword, and I understand why you might be doubting it. There are both advantages and challenges to taking the DIY route, and it often depends on factors like your goals, timeline, resources, and physical capacity. Here's a breakdown of the key considerations, from my perspective:

Advantages of DIYing

1. **Cost Savings:**

   Immediate savings on labor costs is obviously the biggest draw. By doing the work yourself, you can significantly reduce project expenses, allowing you to retain more equity.

2. **Increased Cash Flow Potential:**

   Since DIYing allows you to minimize costs, you get more cashflow and get to take out more money from the refinance, allowing you to reinvest and repeat the process infinitely.

3. **Learning & Control:**

   You learn a lot throughout the process, which can make you feel more in control of the project. Plus, you're able to make decisions on the fly without needing to consult with others. This helps streamline the process (though this depends on your experience and knowledge).

4. **Pride of Work:**

   There's a certain pride in seeing a finished project that you've personally put so much into. That satisfaction can be very motivating, and it also helps you build a deeper connection with the work. However, this is also a con...

Challenges of DIYing

1. **Time Commitment:**

   DIYing is time-consuming—and often much slower than hiring professionals. Construction projects, even for those with experience, can take longer than expected, which can delay timelines and still impact your ROI.

2. **Physical and Mental Toll:**

   DIYing can be physically demanding. This is especially true if you're working long hours, lifting heavy materials, or taking on tasks that are physically exhausting. The mental toll can also be significant, especially when juggling multiple tasks and managing trades on top of everything.

3. **Quality Risks:**

   Without the proper training and experience, the quality of your work could suffer. While YouTube tutorials can be helpful, there's a risk of missing essential steps or overlooking local building codes and permits.

4. **Management Overload:**

   You might underestimate how much time and effort goes into managing multiple aspects of the build, even if you're doing a lot of it yourself. Managing schedules, coordinating with suppliers, and keeping up with deadlines can be just as stressful as the actual physical work, especially if you're balancing a full-time job or other commitments.

5. **Being too connected:**

   In the advantages, I mentioned how being involved in the project makes you develop a deeper connection with the work, but this has a drawback. Being too connected can cause you a lot of anxiety and stress, ultimately affecting your health and your project overall. It's sometimes best to keep an emotional distance from your investments.

6. **Opportunity Cost:**

DIYing means you're spending a lot of time on the project instead of focusing on the growth of your business. If you're not careful, DIYing can prevent you from taking on higher-value projects or building systems that would benefit your long-term success.

In summary, the DIY approach can be cost-effective and deeply rewarding, but it often comes with significant management demands and could negatively impact other areas of your business and your life. This is where the hybrid approach offers an appealing alternative—do some and delegate the rest—letting you retain project control while delegating specialized tasks to skilled professionals.

The Hybrid Approach:

A popular way to do BTR projects, which is the way we do it, is acting as the Project Manager (PM) while hiring out the work to skilled trades. This allows us to take advantage of our expertise in organizing, sourcing materials, and managing timelines, while still getting the professional-level quality and efficiency of experienced tradespeople. This approach saves you from the physical toll but gives you control over the project.

In our first few projects, we were about 50% DIY and 50% hiring trades. Slowly and eventually these numbers started skewing towards 40% DIY, 60% hiring trades. It has since increased to where now we are 10% DIY (managing the build which also includes some hands-on work) and 90% delegation (to trades and to our in-house team). There's less equity in the projects, but we're able to take on more than one build at a time this way, allowing us to scale faster.

My Take:

When someone who has never built before asks me how to start, I always recommend beginning with a small project—like a 2 or 3-unit house-hack, as mentioned in a previous chapter—and aiming for a 30% DIY approach, depending on your skill level of course. If you're very handy and have a good background in construction, you most likely feel confident to take on more. But honestly, whether you take on only 20%

of the DIY or 70% of it, your first project might feel slower than you'd hoped, and that's OK. You need to take the time to learn and maneuver through the project carefully and the hybrid approach is a practical way to go. It will help secure financing, still build some equity, gain hands-on experience, and ease into the process without becoming overwhelmed or discouraged.

As you continue to scale, eventually I think it's important to know when to transition out of DIYing and bring in experts, especially when the workload gets too heavy, or the complexity of the project increases. Especially in areas where specialized skills are required like plumbing, electrical, gas fitting, (etc.) in order to help with your post-build maintenance. It frees up your time, reduces the risk of mistakes, and allows you to focus on scaling your business and maximizing profits. Plus, those specialized trades usually offer warranty on their work for the first year post-build, helping you streamline maintenance.

If you're unsure, you can always experiment with a few tasks that you're comfortable with. I often recommend the finishings, basically anything after the drywall is installed. You could do the painting, install the trim, the floors, the kitchens, the light fixtures, etc. while hiring out for the more complex jobs in the beginning. This can often be a more sustainable approach as you start this business in order to mitigate the risk of taking on too much or creating costly mistakes.

Ultimately, it's about balance—DIYing might make sense for smaller projects or as a temporary strategy, but for large-scale, long-term success, partnering with the right professionals will fuel your business further, ensuring you stay on track and avoid burnout.

In this tip, we focused on the practical side of DIY—when it can work, when it might not, and how to find your footing in your first project. But the full picture of our DIY journey involves more than strategy—it involves burnout, boundaries, and learning when to step back.

For that side of the story, head to Chapter 16, where we dive deeper into what it really took to move from DIYing to HIREing—and why that shift saved our sanity.

TOP THREE TAKEAWAYS:

1. **Leaning on Experts for Guidance:** If you're new to the building process and feel unsure about sequencing or specifics, don't hesitate to ask tradespeople or contractors for advice. They often have the expertise to guide you. Consider shadowing or paying a contractor to answer your questions, or simply dive into the process and learn on the fly.

2. **Avoiding Analysis Paralysis:** While preparation and understanding the process are important, overanalyzing can lead to delays. Embrace the learning curve by getting started, and don't be afraid of making mistakes—they're part of the journey.

3. **DIY as a Learning Tool:** Even if you plan to hire contractors eventually, a hands-on approach in the early stages allows you to gain insight into the process and build confidence. It's also an opportunity to develop relationships with trades and gain valuable knowledge that can be used for better project management in the future.

CHAPTER 14

FIRE AND SOUNDPROOFING

Fireproofing and soundproofing might not be the most exciting parts of a build, but they're absolutely essential in multi-unit construction. They go way beyond just meeting code — they directly impact tenant safety, comfort, and the long-term quality of your building. These are the kinds of details you want to get right from day one, because fixing them after the fact is costly and complicated. Over the years, we've learned what works, what doesn't, and where it's worth investing a bit more upfront.

FIREPROOFING: SAFETY FIRST

Fireproofing involves using materials and methods, such as fire-rated building materials and sprinkler systems, to slow down or prevent the spread of fire between units. It's obviously very important for ensuring tenant safety, complying with local building codes, and protecting your investment.

KEY FIREPROOFING STRATEGIES

1. **Fire-Rated Materials**: Use fire-resistant materials such as Type X drywall, concrete blocks, and fire-rated insulation. These materials are designed to withstand high temperatures and provide vital time for evacuation.

2. **Compartmentalization**: Your draftsman should design the building to include fire-resistant compartments with fire-rated

floors, ceilings, and walls to contain fires within specific areas. For example, a garage bay will have a fire-rated door to access the inside of the house, a fire-rated wall composition between itself and the inside of the house and it needs to be drywalled and taped on the inside of its walls and ceiling. This makes the garage its own compartment. The same principal would apply with each apartment unit.

3. **Fire Doors and Seals**: Each 'compartment' needs its own fire-rated door with a self-closing mechanism. All gaps must be sealed with fire-resistant caulk or intumescent sealants to prevent the spread of flames and smoke.

4. **Sprinkler Systems**: Depending on the building code and local municipal regulation, automatic sprinkler systems may be needed throughout the building. These systems are highly effective in suppressing fires before they can spread. In our case we've never had to install them since code only requires them for larger or more commercial builds.

5. **Fire-Stopping Penetrations**: You will probably need fire-stopping materials to seal gaps around pipes, ducts, and electrical conduits that pass through walls and floors. These penetrations can act as conduits for fire if left untreated.

6. **Fire Alarms and Detection Systems**: Most building codes require a fire detection system, like smoke detectors. Here, the code is pretty extensive on them. It requires one on each level of each unit, including the basement and in each bedroom as well. They must be interconnected, hard-wired with a battery back up and must have an integrated strobe light for individuals who are deaf or hard of hearing.

FIREPROOFING STANDARDS AND COMPLIANCE

Ensure all fireproofing measures meet local building codes and fire safety regulations. For instance, the Ontario Building Code (OBC) requires specific fire ratings for walls, floors, and ceilings in multi-unit buildings.

Fire ratings are measured in hours (e.g., 1-hour or 2-hour fire rating), indicating how long a material or assembly can resist fire before structural integrity is compromised. For example:

- **1-Hour Fire Rating**: Walls or floors can contain fire for one hour, allowing time for evacuation and emergency response.

- **2-Hour Fire Rating**: Offers greater protection and is typically required for critical areas such as stairwells and exit corridors.

We spent a lot of time on this subject during our college studies in architectural technology. Your draftsman will be able to guide you in understanding what's involved in your local regulations and building code to ensure your build is compliant and safe.

PRACTICAL FIREPROOFING TIPS

- Use Type X drywall (we always install two layers of the thicker ⅝" type X), which provides a longer fire rating.

- Incorporate Rockwool or other fire-rated insulation into walls and ceilings.

- All the materials must be well installed to maintain the integrity of the fire-rated assemblies.

BUILDING TO PROTECT FROM WILDFIRES

In addition to traditional fireproofing strategies, you should consider taking measures to protect your buildings from the increasing threat of wildfires. Wildfire-resistant construction involves using materials and design strategies that minimize the risk of ignition from flying embers, direct flames, and intense radiant heat.

Here are some key wildfire-resilient construction techniques:

- **Fire-Resistant Roofing**: Utilizing Class A-rated roofing materials like metal, clay tiles, or asphalt shingles can enhance the building's resistance to fires. Sealing any gaps in the roof and eaves is essential to prevent embers from entering.

- **Siding and Exterior Walls**: Choosing non-combustible materials such as fiber cement, stucco, or metal for exterior walls can help. Avoid using untreated wood or vinyl siding, as these can easily ignite or melt under extreme heat.

- **Defensible Space**: Creating a defensible space around the building involves clearing out vegetation and other flammable materials within at least 30 feet. Fire-resistant landscaping options like gravel or stone ground cover can also help reduce fuel for wildfires.

- **Fire-Resistant Decks and Fences**: Construct decks and fences using non-combustible materials. For wood components, using fire-resistant coatings or pressure-treated options rated for fire safety is recommended.

- **Windows and Doors**: Installing tempered glass windows and fire-rated exterior doors can improve fire protection. Adding metal screens to vents can help prevent embers from entering.

- **Fire Barriers and Sprinklers**: External fire barriers, like firewalls, can help slow the spread of flames, especially in areas prone to wildfires. Incorporating a sprinkler system throughout the building can aid in controlling fire spread.

- **Access and Egress**: Designing wide driveways and pathways ensures easy access for emergency vehicles and facilitates safe evacuation for residents during wildfire events.

These measures are particularly critical in regions prone to wildfires or where climate change has heightened the risk. It may help reduce your insurance premium significantly while increasing the resilience of your property to natural disasters and ensuring tenant safety. Although, if you're located in a zone prone to wildfires, your building code might have already adapted and added a few extra requirements.

SOUNDPROOFING: THE TENANT EXPERIENCE

Soundproofing focuses on reducing the noise that travels between units using materials that absorb sound frequencies and vibrations in the floor/

ceiling compositions and in the party walls. Effective soundproofing is vital for tenant satisfaction and can significantly impact the success of your investment. Poor soundproofing can lead to tenant complaints, high turnover rates, disputes, neglected units, and even decreased rent payments. Even in new buildings with desirable amenities, inadequate soundproofing could lead to rent reductions within the first few years just to retain tenants.

KEY SOUNDPROOFING TIPS:

- **Plan Ahead**: Discuss soundproofing strategies with your draftsman during the initial consultation to ensure it is integrated into the overall design.

- **Plan Areas Wisely**: Avoid placing high-traffic areas like entrances and kitchens directly above bedrooms. Ideally, place bedrooms over other bedrooms when possible. Design common spaces such as hallways and stairways with sound-absorbing materials like acoustic panels to minimize noise transmission.

- **Use Soundproofing Materials**: Incorporate materials like acoustic panels, foam, or mass-loaded vinyl in walls, ceilings, and floors to enhance soundproofing.

- **Add Soundproofing Insulation**: Use insulation such as fiberglass, Rockwool, or cellulose to further improve soundproofing. Ensure the insulation material is compatible with other materials.

- **Use Soundproof Doors**: Specify solid core doors with weather stripping to prevent sound from entering or escaping through doorways.

- **Seal Gaps and Cracks**: Seal all gaps and cracks around windows, doors, electrical outlets, and other openings with silicone caulk or acoustic sealant to prevent sound leaks.

- **Address HVAC Noise**: Incorporate soundproofing measures in your HVAC design, such as using a soundproof system or insulating ducts and pipes to reduce noise transmission.

While there are various soundproofing options available, the highest-grade soundproofing is often achieved through cement construction. This involves using precast cement floors and block walls, as it provides excellent sound isolation due to their density and mass. However, this method is obviously way more expensive and not the norm for small multi-unit investments.

For those of us small builders seeking simple stick-framing sound proof solutions, keep reading. But first, you might want to understand the basic math behind it...

UNDERSTANDING STC

STC (Sound Transmission Class) is a rating that measures how effectively a building material or assembly blocks airborne sound. The higher the STC rating, the better the material is at reducing sound transmission. STC is measured by testing how much sound is blocked across a range of frequencies, from low bass sounds (like traffic or machinery) to higher-pitched noises (like voices or alarms).

Here's a breakdown of STC ratings:

- **STC 30-39**: Normal conversation is easily heard through the wall or floor.

- **STC 40-49**: Loud speech is audible but somewhat muffled.

- **STC 50-59**: Most sounds are significantly reduced, making conversations difficult to hear.

- **STC 60 and above**: Starting from most sounds being inaudible or faint, and ranging to completely soundproof (if above 60).

In multi-unit buildings, high STC ratings in floors, walls, and ceilings are crucial for tenant comfort and privacy. Our current floor system, with insulation, resilient channels, and acoustic panels, achieves an STC rating of around 60. This provides excellent soundproofing and significantly reduces noises from footsteps, conversations, or other activities.

ESTIMATING STC RATINGS

Most Building Codes, including the Ontario Building Code (OBC), provide tables with STC and fire ratings for various assembly options, which can guide you in choosing effective wall and floor compositions. Your designer or engineer can help you navigate these resources. However, here's a simplified approach if you want to estimate the STC rating of a floor or wall system on your own.

1. **List All Materials in the Assembly**: Identify each material in your floor or wall system—such as vinyl flooring, subfloor, resilient channels, drywall, and insulation. Each material's density and structure contribute to the overall soundproofing performance.

2. **Review Material STC Ratings**: Manufacturers often provide soundproofing data for individual materials, giving a baseline of how much sound they can block. While STC ratings aren't directly additive, each layer's properties help determine the final rating.

3. **Estimate Based on Key Components**:

   ↳ **Mass**: Adding mass with dense materials (e.g., Advantech subfloor or concrete) typically increases the STC by reducing airborne sound transmission.

   ↳ **Resilient Channels and Insulation**: Resilient channels reduce structural vibrations, while sound-absorbing insulation blocks airborne noise. These can improve the STC by approximately 10-15 points.

   ↳ **Acoustic Panels**: Panels like Sonopan add sound absorption, further raising the STC, particularly in blocking high-frequency sounds.

For example, starting with a basic assembly with an STC of around 30:

• Adding Advantech subfloor and/or lightweight concrete could add ten points.

• Including resilient channels and Rockwool insulation might add another 15 points.

- Adding an acoustic layer (e.g., Sonopan) could contribute an additional five points.

Together, this could yield an estimated STC of around 60. Remember: Factors like construction quality and installation techniques can greatly affect performance. You need to catch all the cracks to make it effective. But now that you understand the boring math behind it, we can move on to more practical information.

FLOOR COMPOSITIONS

The primary source of sound transfer in multi-unit buildings typically occurs between floors and ceilings. Footstep vibrations from above can significantly disturb tenants below. Effective separation layers in the structure are essential to mitigate low-frequency noise.

Here's our refined approach after years of experimentation— designed to save you from trial and error. I'll start by sharing how we began, followed by what our current composition looks like today.

OUR <u>ORIGINAL</u> FLOOR COMPOSITION:

- **LVP (Luxury Vinyl Plank) Flooring**
- **Foam Underlay**
- **½ inch Aspenite**
- **1 Layer of Safe N Sound Insulation** (between floor joists) to block high-frequency noises.
- **Resilient Metal Channels** every 16 inches to absorb low-frequency vibrations.
- **2 Layers of 5/8" Type X Drywall**

This setup offered some soundproofing with an STC rating of about 52 and a 1-hour fire rating, but heavy footsteps and other noises were still audible.

OUR <u>CURRENT</u> FLOOR COMPOSITION:

- **LVP flooring with integrated underlay**
- **Advantech Subflooring** (instead of ½ inch aspenite), which is dense and moisture-resistant.
- **Squeak-Proof Glue** applied on joists before installing Advantech.
- **Blown Cellulose Insulation** in floor joists instead of batt insulation.
- **Acoustic Panels** (e.g., Sonopan) between joists and resilient channels.
- **Resilient Channels** spaced at 16 inches.
- **2 Layers of 5/8" Type X Drywall**

We now use Advantech subflooring instead of ½" aspenite because it is made from compressed wood fibers bonded with resin, creating a dense, moisture-resistant panel that offers superior strength and durability compared to traditional plywood or OSB (Oriented Strand Board). It resists swelling, warping, and delamination, even when exposed to moisture. We also put squeak-proof glue on top of the joists before installing the Advantech.

Additionally, we add a layer of acoustic panels like Sonopan between the joists and resilient channels. A couple times too we've done blown cellulose insulation instead of batt insulation between the floor joists, which, Rob thought, improved the rating. I'm not convinced it made that big of a difference though. It also creates a mess if you ever have to open up the ceiling for repairs.

Our current floor composition has improved soundproofing performance from our old composition, with an STC rating of about **60 and a 1.5-hour fire rating**, offering much greater tenant comfort.

Lightweight concrete is another option we're finally testing out— and it should take soundproofing between units to the next level. We've never used it before, mainly because of the hefty price tag that comes with it. But for our current joint venture 6-plex, the numbers made sense to support the added cost, so we figured it was time to try it. The idea is that pouring a thin slab of lightweight concrete over the subfloor adds mass and density, which helps reduce airborne and impact noise between floors. We'll let you know if it's worth the extra $10K once the build is done—stay tuned on Instagram for updates.

No matter the set up you choose, achieving high soundproofing performance is highly dependent on proper installation. It's crucial to ensure that the assembly is continuous throughout, especially beneath stairs and landings.

PARTY WALL OR COMMON WALL COMPOSITIONS:

In multi-unit buildings, "party" or "common walls" are the walls that separate individual units. Properly constructing these walls is crucial for minimizing sound transfer and ensuring tenant privacy. We have developed a multi-layered construction process designed to maximize soundproofing.

1. **Two separate 2x4 walls (or two 2x6):** Usually the longest middle wall between the living area of the units you want to maximize the sound proofing, so we'll frame either two 2x4 walls, but usually it's two 2x6 walls for structural purposes. They are framed one next to each other with a 1 inch gap in between.

2. **Staggered 2x4 Walls:** Or sometimes, in tight spaces or in between a shared staircase maybe, we have built 2x4 stud walls that are staggered on a 2x6 plate, positioned so they do not directly connect. This staggered construction creates a physical separation that helps prevent sound from traveling directly through the wall structure.

3. **Insulation:** The walls are filled with fire-rated, soundproofing insulation, such as Rockwool or fiberglass. This insulation serves as a barrier to absorb and block sound waves, particularly high-frequency noises like voices.

4. **Drywall:** We apply two layers of 5/8" Type X drywall on each side of the walls. Type X drywall is specifically designed to enhance fire resistance and soundproofing. The double layers add mass and create additional sound barriers, further reducing noise transmission.

Alternative Approach:

- **Block Walls**: In some cases, incorporating concrete or block walls in addition to the staggered 2x4 construction can further enhance soundproofing. While block walls offer excellent mass and sound isolation, they can also reduce interior space and increase construction costs.

If you don't have the budget nor the space for block walls, I recommend doing the two walls framed next to another as opposed to just the staggered wall. It has proven to be the most effective solution without breaking the bank or the usable space. Even though it does reduce interior space a little, its benefits in soundproofing and tenant satisfaction definitely outweigh that slight drawback.

TIP: Don't forget to check local building codes or if the municipality has any additional requirements.

CHAPTER 15

THE ART OF PROJECT MANAGEMENT & WORKING WITH TRADES

Let's be real—if your project management isn't solid, things will fall apart fast. Delays, miscommunication, missed steps... it adds up. That's why having a clear plan and someone capable leading the charge is key.

By now you've probably picked up on the fact that one of the biggest reasons we've been able to pull this off is because we self-manage our builds instead of handing them over to a turn-key builder. So if you're planning to take a similar approach, this chapter is one you don't want to skip.

Being a good project manager isn't just about checking off a to-do list. You need to understand the technical stuff, be good with people, and know how to think on your feet—especially when things don't go as planned (because they won't). Let's dive into what makes a great project manager and how to keep your build running as smoothly as possible.

REQUESTING THE REQUIRED DOCUMENTS

The first thing to do when hiring trades, other than requesting estimates and references, is to request proof of their legal business documents. These documents vary depending on the regulations in your area, but they could include licenses, insurance documents, or mandatory worker's compensation insurance information. Here in Ontario, the trades need liability insurance and WSIB insurance (a provincial worker's mandatory compensation insurance).

As a builder, even with owner-built homes, we need to make sure trades have that insurance. Otherwise, if the Ministry of Labour or the Ministry of Health and Safety does a surprise inspection on our site and finds a trade that is not registered with WSIB, whoever's in charge of the job site can be fined. Before hiring a trade, research the legally required documents in your area, verify that the trades have them, and request a copy for your records. This will help ensure that your job site is in compliance with the law, and that your trades are protected in the event of an accident on the job site.

ENSURING SAFETY PROCEDURES

As the project manager, you are responsible for ensuring that all work meets the necessary building permit requirements, safety regulations, PPE conditions (Personal Protective Equipment like construction hats, steel toe boots, etc.), and any other standards set by local authorities. You'll need to be sure that safety procedures are in place. The Ministry of Labour in Ontario requires all construction sites to have specific documents pinned on a board and remain on site during the length of the construction like the permits, safety posters, a map to the nearest hospital, and other specific forms. We also need to have a fire extinguisher and medical kit on site.

To be compliant, we use a sheet of plywood (usually about 4x4 ish) and staple all the required papers to the sheet, making sure they remain visible on site and keeping the fire extinguisher and medical kit nearby. And yes, we have had to use the fire extinguisher on site before... that was a scary day. To streamline the process, research the requirements you will have to abide by and develop a straightforward procedure for maintaining compliance.

If you're wondering about the scary day with the fire extinguisher—here's the story. During one of our builds, a propane tank caught fire while the masons were installing exterior stone. It was February, minus 20°C, and they had tarped and heated a corner of the building to warm the area for the install. Somehow, one of the tank's valves ignited. Rob was working on the second floor when he looked out the window and saw the masons panicking. He bolted down the half-built stairs, grabbed the fire extinguisher, and ran straight toward the flames… only to realize after the fact that it may not have been the safest move. But thankfully, he managed to put out the fire and save the building. We thanked our lucky stars that the tank didn't explode while he was near it. In hindsight, the smarter move would have been to call the fire department and clear the area—but when you're in the middle of it, instincts kick in.

PROVIDING NECESSARY FACILITIES

You also must prepare the site with basic facilities such as a toilet and a designated area for waste and excess materials. We make sure to have a toilet readily available early on from the excavation phase. If need be, we move it around as the job progresses. Having a toilet that's easy to get to at all times on site will avoid unpleasant practices like the use of makeshift alternatives such as empty boxes or bottles. We've heard all kinds of stories… Such practices will only burden you with a dirty mess to clear.

Before too, we wanted to minimize expenses so we would keep a dump trailer on site for waste management instead of renting bins from companies. You can have a designated person, such as the project manager or an employee, in charge of emptying the trailer at a landfill site when it gets full. That does require more effort than relying on a rental bin, but you can save money and prevent the accumulation of waste if the trailer is emptied frequently. You don't want the site to always look messy to people driving by, as that can give you a bad reputation. And it helps keep the site safe. Ideally though, you work a rental bin in the budget so your PM can keep focused on higher priority tasks.

BEING PROACTIVE

I could probably write a whole chapter on the importance of being proactive in construction. Back when I worked as a home designer, I'd occasionally visit the sites where we had designed the house or building. One site still sticks with me — a triplex in the heart of Ottawa. The project manager would show up, park across the street, and spend the entire day in his truck. He claimed he was "managing" things from there. Meanwhile, I'd hear the trades openly vent about how absent he was. Not surprisingly, that site was riddled with problems. It really showed me that being a good project manager isn't about barking orders from a distance — it's about being present and engaged so you can catch issues before they snowball.

Now, I'm not saying you need to follow the trades around or live on-site. But checking in daily — sometimes multiple times a day — and physically walking the site makes a massive difference. For example, there was one time we were pouring a foundation, and the structural engineer had specified that the footings along the side walls needed to be thirty inches wide, while the rest were twenty-four. The crew installing the forms didn't catch that detail and prepped the entire perimeter at twenty-four inches. Rob stopped by after they left and noticed the mistake. With the cement truck en route and the crew already off to another job, he and another guy grabbed hammers and adjusted the forms themselves. It only took a few minutes, but it saved us from delaying the pour and pulling a crew back. That kind of hands-on, proactive approach keeps projects moving and problems minimal. I doubt the guy sitting in his truck across the street would have noticed that.

In most situations, it's best to call the trades back to complete their work properly—especially when it's a specialized trade, and you want their warranty to cover it. When they can return promptly, that's ideal. But sometimes, waiting isn't an option.

When that happens, Rob has been known to take matters into his own hands. I've seen him rent equipment and watch YouTube tutorials to find solutions on the spot when waiting for a trade would have caused significant delays. This can be crucial when the next trades and material deliveries are already scheduled.

For example, during the Covid-19 pandemic, when construction permits were all released at once after the first lockdown, foundation crews were overwhelmed and facing major delays. This worried us since it was August, and in Canada, the construction season is short when you're trying to beat winter. When our foundation crew finally poured the concrete, they told us they couldn't say when they'd be back to install the waterproofing membrane.

Rather than waiting indefinitely, Rob researched the process, bought the materials, and did it himself. A few days later, we backfilled, received our lumber delivery, and the framers got started. As a result, our project moved forward much faster than others in the area, who were delayed several weeks waiting for that same step.

That said, I don't necessarily recommend this. If we ever have moisture issues in that particular basement, we won't have a warranty on that work. But sometimes, you have to do what you have to do to keep things moving, especially when you're racing Mother Nature.

Taking on the "gray area work," as mentioned later in this chapter, is also a valuable example of being efficient and proactive.

PROBLEM-SOLVING

Problem-solving is a significant part of being a project manager, and something that is very difficult to master but comes gradually with experience. As the one in charge, you will be the go-to person for the trades when they encounter any issues, big or small, or when they have any kind of question. Your role is to find solutions to problems that arise during the build. This is why having some construction experience is valuable, as the problems you will face may not be as simple as pointing out where you want the light fixture to be installed. You can find yourself addressing more technical or complex issues. You need to understand construction techniques, materials, and processes; provide guidance and solutions based on your expertise; and collaborate effectively with architects, engineers, and subcontractors.

If you need clarification on something, seek help from various sources. Can the trade offer advice that is based on their experience? Can you search for information online? Are there any relevant building codes you can refer to? Can you consult with another experienced builder? As a project manager, it's your responsibility to find a way to manage and solve all the problems.

MANAGING THE "GRAY AREA" WORK

Lastly, I want to talk about the "gray area work," which is a term I came up with to describe tasks that fall between the responsibilities of two different trades. It often involves work that serves as a bridge between two separate trades but can lead to confusion about who is responsible for its completion. For instance, one trade may claim that it's not their job, while the other may say that the previous trade should have done the work. This leads to the ball being passed back and forth between trades, with extra fees added to the budget as a result. To avoid this, our in-house guys (and Rob) does a lot of the "gray area work" themselves. But when you don't have a team, an even better solution is to assign these tasks to the trades ahead of time.

An example of "gray area work" is installing the moisture barrier membrane after framing. Some framers may do it as they construct the walls, but they may charge extra when they assume it's the exterior finisher's job. Meanwhile, the exterior finisher might assume it was the farmer's job, but they'll also offer to do it for an extra fee.

Another example is bulkhead framing. If there are bulkheads in your build, someone will need to frame them and prepare them for the drywaller. Because this job is done after the framing and after the mechanical work, who will do this? Will you make the framer come back for this or assign it to the drywaller's lists of duties? Or will you as the PM frame them or ask your general labor to do it?

With experience, you start to assign all those little "gray area" tasks to the right trades ahead of time—and build them into the budget. But like most people learning the ropes, you'll probably manage things as they come up. It's tough to catch every small detail in advance. The key is being prepared to step in and handle them yourself when needed.

EFFICIENCY IN MIND

According to Rob, efficiency equals money. He strongly emphasizes efficiency and is constantly focused on finding ways to make the job run smoother. His dedication to efficiency can even be annoying when he uses that same mindset in personal or family settings. However, his thinking process of "What can I do to improve efficiency?" is something to strive for. The waterproofing membrane example I mentioned is a good illustration of this.

It's equally important to consider efficiency in small details, such as printing out the most recent plans and specs before meeting a trade on site to prevent mistakes. Or making sure the site is organized, clean, and has all the necessary material there and ready for that next trade. The more you embrace this mindset, the more natural it becomes, and efficiency eventually becomes second nature.

EFFECTIVE PLANNING SKILLS

Planning is something else that every project manager needs to do effectively, but planning is a skill that comes with experience. Figuring out and providing what the next trade may need from you to help them do their jobs sets them up for success, which ultimately causes you to succeed. For instance, if you are supplying bathtub and shower units, make sure they are delivered and brought inside the work area before the plumbers arrive. If any other crew members have left a mess, tidy up the space to give the next crew enough room to work.

Ensure you have the latest version of all plans and specs, such as the construction drawings and the supplier's kitchen and bath designs. You can print and even laminate the key pages and staple them to their corresponding walls. That makes it easy for everyone to understand that, let's say, the vanity is to be installed along a specific wall, and the pipes need to be installed at a specific distance. Even if you're simply meeting the electrical crew for an on-site walk-through before they start, you need to have the electrical plans available showing where all the lights, plugs and important fixtures are going. Having this kind of information readily available can reduce potential mistakes.

We also try to encourage all the workers to clean up after themselves at the end of each day, but we found that the only way to keep up that momentum is if the job site was already tidy when they arrived. Whatever makes their jobs easier. This is actually a big part of the job of our in-house labor. Obviously if you don't have full-time help, you could put an ad on social media to find a student or someone looking for a few extra hours of work every week, and put them in charge of tidying the site and taking care of the garbage. If the workers can spend that extra hour working on the job instead of needing to clean, it helps the project move along faster. Just make sure you have proper insurance in place to cover students and unofficial trade workers of this sort.

EFFICIENT SCHEDULING

Careful scheduling is key to keeping your project running smoothly. Ideally, you want to avoid having multiple trades working on top of each other—it creates chaos and slows everyone down. But in reality, things don't always go as planned. Sometimes a crew says they'll be there Monday, but they don't show up until Thursday… and now they're overlapping with the next trade you had booked. Suddenly the site is a mess.

The best you can do is try to stagger your trades. Aim to have one crew on site at a time, and give the next one a heads-up to be ready a few days later. That gives you room to confirm timelines and adjust on the fly, reducing the risk of conflicts and keeping the workflow more manageable.

You can however, consider sending masons or exterior finishing crews while you have trades working inside, since they should work in different areas and won't interfere with each other. Typically, we try to limit the number of trades working on site to two at any given time, as this makes management easier and reduces the likelihood of errors or conflicts.

Another scenario where careful planning is crucial is when you're working on a tight site with limited parking and close neighbors. Neighbors are rarely supportive of disruptive construction crews, especially if they're taking up street parking or blocking driveways.

TIP: Before booking a trade, schedule an on-site walk-through with them a few weeks in advance. This gives them a clear sense of the scope and allows them to flag anything they'll need from you—or from the site—to get their job done efficiently. Otherwise, if the site isn't at par with their needs, they will leave to go work on another job site instead, creating delays and scheduling conflicts for your site.

QUALITY CONTROL

A good project manager needs to keep an eye on quality control. Skimping on materials and workmanship might save money upfront, but it can lead to expensive repairs and maintenance down the road. This applies not only to the materials but also to the contractors you hire—and maintaining good communication with them is key. Hiring contractors without proper vetting or choosing them solely based on price can result in poor work quality, missed deadlines, and conflict. It's also important to keep track of all changes, decisions, and conversations to avoid misunderstandings later. And when it comes to your budget, stay on top of expenses, look for cost-effective solutions, and tackle any budget overruns quickly and honestly.

HAVING THE RIGHT ATTITUDE

As a project manager, communication is everything. You've got to stay respectful, keep your cool, and show up with a positive, solutions-focused mindset. At the same time, you need to keep things moving—so a bit of urgency helps too.

Be humble. Be open to learning from the people around you. But also, don't be afraid to speak up when something doesn't sit right. If you feel strongly about something, say it—just say it in a way that keeps the relationship intact.

I know that sounds like a lot to balance, but with time, it becomes second nature. That mix of confidence and curiosity goes a long way in earning the respect of your trades and building relationships that last.

One trick we use all the time: we ask for input. Something like, "In your experience, what's the best way to handle this?" It shows you respect their expertise, but still keeps you in the driver's seat.

Building strong relationships is essential—something you can achieve by showing empathy and respect. And trust me, these connections *are* important! Relationships are everything in this business. In any business for that matter. Or else, good luck building an empire all by yourself.

WORKING WITH INSPECTORS

Dealing with inspectors can be frustrating at times. Every seasoned contractor has likely faced a situation where a new inspector arrives on-site, and suddenly there's a disagreement about code interpretation. It's a common complaint I've heard from builders and trades alike:

"That guy doesn't know what he's talking about! I never had a problem with the last inspector." or *"How can someone who spends most of their time in an office reading the code — but hasn't done the actual work — suddenly show up and tell me how to do the job I've been doing for years?"*

We've been there too, and it's incredibly frustrating when it happens.

When these situations arise, it's crucial to remain calm and professional, no matter how frustrating it may feel. However, emotions can get the better of us, as we experienced during a final occupancy inspection of one of our triplexes in early 2024.

The issue involved a stair landing adjoining the entrance door of a basement unit. The previous inspector had approved the framing of said landing with the way it connected to the door sill, since due to the wall composition and the way the building was designed, it couldn't be resolved in any other way. The previous inspector had used her experience and common sense to recognize that the design posed no safety risk despite not perfectly meeting the code, and passed our inspection. Unfortunately, this inspector moved on to another job before the project was completed, and a new inspector took over.

When it came time for the final Occupancy inspection, the new inspector interpreted the same landing differently, classifying the door sill as a step and insisting on a correction. This would have required us to undo and rebuild an entire section of the completed building, just days before our tenants moved-in. Rob attempted to explain the situation and tried to offer alternative solutions or request that the inspector offer alternative solutions to achieve compliance without needing such drastic measures. The inspector, however, dismissed Rob's concerns, stating it wasn't the inspector's job to help find solutions.

Tensions flared, and the conversation ended abruptly. Nothing frustrates us more than when the other side refuses to listen, or to even try to incorporate a little common sense into a discussion. Frustrated by the lack of collaboration and the unreasonable demand, we knew we needed a different approach. That evening, we gathered our facts and composed a professional email to the Chief Building Official (CBO). We outlined the situation, included references to the building code and requested a review. The next morning, I met with the CBO in person to discuss the matter.

I calmly explained that, over our ten years of building within this municipality, we had consistently maintained positive relationships with the officials and intended to continue doing so. I respectfully requested that the new inspector be removed from our projects for the time being. Additionally, I asked the CBO to review the compliance issue and consult with other professionals, emphasizing that redoing an entire section of the completed building and delaying our tenant's move-in by over a month or so at the last minute was not a reasonable solution. Especially since this issue had already been passed and accepted by the previous city official.

After reviewing the facts and the situation, the CBO issued a Passed Inspection report and temporarily reassigned the inspector from our projects. During my discussion with the CBO, I had emphasized the importance of inspectors working collaboratively with contractors to achieve the shared goal of compliance. When an inspector refuses to engage constructively and creates unnecessary tension, it hinders progress and leads to negative outcomes for everyone involved.

The lesson here is that professionalism and clear communication are essential when dealing with inspectors. While it can be tempting to react emotionally in the heat of the moment, taking a step back to present your case calmly and constructively is far more effective. If an inspector remains uncooperative, remember that you can always escalate the matter to a superior to seek resolution. Building strong, respectful relationships with officials is invaluable, but it's equally important to stand your ground when necessary—always with courtesy and professionalism.

TIP: Keeping detailed records is essential, but during construction, it can be challenging to document every little detail. I recommend exploring project management cloud-based apps that make it easy to document and organize everything. Personally, we only use OneDrive with a well-structured filing system to keep everything in one place. The importance is to have those apps installed on your phone and those of your employees if any, making it convenient to document and save important information as efficiently as possible.

WORKING WITH NEIGHBORS

Honestly, I could dedicate an entire chapter to the stories about our dealings with neighbors, and it would be quite entertaining. But since this book isn't focused on that, I'll keep it to a couple of short anecdotes, both for entertainment purposes and as a heads-up. I'd rather you brace yourself for the potential drama than do your first build, experience major drama and tell me I should have warned you beforehand. Consider this your fair warning: Neighbors *don't* like developers.

The reality is that most people don't like change. The idea of new neighbors—especially renters, thanks to negative stereotypes—makes them nervous. If you're building next to them, it's often on land that was either vacant and peaceful, or an old, possibly abandoned house that had become part of the quiet charm of the neighborhood. Then, suddenly, you show up with bulldozers, noise, and disruption.

I can understand their concerns. But here's the thing: If they didn't want disruption, maybe they should have done their homework on becoming savvy investors — like reading this book — and bought the lot themselves. While I know that's not realistic for most people, I don't blame them for being concerned; I blame the way they handle it. There's always a right way to respond to uncertainty, but unfortunately, many people let their emotions take over and choose the wrong way. So, be prepared for pushback, complaints, outbursts, harassment — and yes, even threats. We've seen it all.

We once bought an old house that had been abandoned for years. It was infested with bats, rats, and raccoons. The backyard was overgrown with trees, so we hired a crew to clear it out before starting demolition. At first, the neighbors were friendly, even offering to cut the grass for us. But when a branch fell on their gutter and dented it, things took a turn.

The crew was ready to replace the gutter, but before they could even make the offer, the neighbors exploded—yelling, threatening, and even making death threats. When Rob went to check on the site the next day, he faced the same hostility. As much as he wanted to yell back or call the cops, he kept his cool. He knew we were in for a 6-8 month project, and starting off with a "shit show" wouldn't help anyone.

Rob calmly promised to replace the gutter and assured them we'd be mindful during construction. At the same time, he laid down boundaries: They were not to approach our crews without our consent. Any concerns were to be addressed directly with him, and we'd be installing security fencing and cameras to monitor the site.

The conversation ended on a relatively positive note, but the problem didn't stop there. On the day before the demolition, she threatened to "send someone after Rob" if the dust from the demo harmed her interior birds. I swear you can't make this stuff up. Then, just after we demo'd the house, she stormed out and started screaming, cursing and threatening our excavator guy for making too much noise—we even have it on video.

To finally shut it down, Rob went over one evening and calmly explained that if we heard another word out of her, we'd be calling the cops immediately. This behaviour was harassment and we would not tolerate it for one second longer. The threat of police was enough to scare her into silence. Rob ended the conversation on a friendly note, handing over his business card and telling her that if she ever had a *valid* concern, she could respectfully call him, and he'd look for solutions. We haven't had an issue with those neighbors since. She's even incredibly friendly and helpful now.

Rob did good because honestly, I was ready to throw down. His calm, firm approach kept things professional, saved us months of unnecessary drama, and kept the project on track. Unfortunately, handling conflict as a PM is sometimes just as big of a task than handling the actual construction.

We usually take the time to knock on neighbors' doors and introduce ourselves at the start of a build. It shows that we're not just some faceless corporation—we're people who care about the community. We offer our business cards and ask that any concerns be brought directly to us so we can address them. This often helps, though it's never perfect.

Years ago, we had a neighbor from a few houses down storm into our building while Rob was working. She was furious because we'd chosen the same gray siding as her newly renovated house — never mind that her place was tucked behind large trees, and we hadn't even noticed it. I'd picked the color based on a previous build we'd done, but she was convinced we'd copied her, and she made it clear she hated us for it. She also made sure we knew that no one on the street liked us for building a fourplex there. How dare we make use of an unused field!

Months later, after the build was finished and tenanted, we got a long email from another neighbor on that same street — this one claiming to speak for several others. Their list of complaints included things like a tenant's garbage blowing away on a windy day (even though it was properly placed at the curb for collection), a tenant using their snowmobile on a Friday afternoon, and my personal favorite: A tenant being "rude" after a neighbor yelled at him for washing his car with a noisy pressure washer...at 2 p.m. on a Wednesday. Of course, my tenant was rude! Good for him.

It was clear they were grasping at straws to find reasons to complain. We wrote a polite email saying that all of our tenants were within their rights, advised them to never step foot on our property again without an invitation, and told them that any of these complaints should have been directed to the local By-Law officers. Knowing too well that the By-Law officers would dismiss this nonsense. We also made it clear that this would be their last communication with us, and with our tenants. And sure enough, we never heard from them again.

At the end of the day, no matter how unreasonable people may seem, staying calm, setting boundaries, and focusing on solutions is what gets you through — because in this business, you can't afford to let every complaint or conflict throw you off track. Which brings me to my next point...

CONFLICT RESOLUTION

I want to give conflict resolution its own section because I think it's important. Conflict is something that no one can avoid, unfortunately. As soon as you work and interact with other human beings, especially when you are managing people, conflict is inevitable. Obviously, the goal as a PM is to reduce the number of conflicts or to try to avoid them altogether, but when something does come up, it's extremely important to deal with it professionally.

Priority number 1 of most conflicting situations in business is to take the emotions out of the equation. In both construction and tenant management, emotions can cloud judgment and hinder decision-making. Initially, our emotional investment in every project was strong. However, as our business grew, it became evident that emotions had no place in efficient business management.

We once had a fallout with a civil engineering firm due to concerns over their lack of progress despite charging us substantial fees. Frustration was building, but before responding to their latest email — one that really pushed our buttons — we took a step back. We waited a few days to cool down, removed emotions from the equation, and focused on the facts. Once ready, we gathered our timeline of events and used ChatGPT to draft a professional yet firm email.

Ultimately, we parted ways with the firm. Tensions were high, but we made an effort to leave on a somewhat professional note. While we don't plan on ever going back to them — since going to another firm turned out to be the best decision — you can't always predict the future. If we ever find ourselves needing their help again, we'd rather not have the door slammed in our faces.

It's not about winning or losing a conflict, it's about protecting your reputation and your relationships. Burning bridges is risky, unnecessary, and frankly, uncomfortable. You don't know if you might ever need something from that person or run into them in a different setting. Stay calm, stick to the facts, and try to be polite — that's what professionalism looks like.

AVOIDING CONFLICTS OF INTEREST

Our experience has taught us that it's always best to avoid hiring family members, close friends, and especially tenants—or really anyone who could present a potential conflict of interest. While we do make occasional exceptions, such as hiring a few trusted close friends or family members who have consistently proven their reliability, we approach these situations with caution. We always establish clear boundaries and mutual understanding before entering into any working relationship.

However, when it comes to tenants, we are particularly strict about not hiring them. From past experiences, we've learned that mixing the tenant/landlord relationship with a hired-help/boss dynamic can lead to significant problems. Both relationships—tenant/landlord and hired-help/boss—require clear rules and guidelines to function properly. Blurring these boundaries almost always results in complications.

Once, early in our investment journey, we made the mistake of allowing a tenant—let's call him Bob—to take on a project for us. Bob lived in one of our early single-family homes, and he expressed interest in finishing the basement for himself. At the time, we hadn't planned to finish the basement anytime soon, but he offered to do it if we supplied all the material. We figured it was a good opportunity. We agreed, thinking it would be a win-win: He would get the space he wanted, and we'd get added equity for free labour.

However, despite receiving the materials we provided for the project, Bob barely made any progress. Months passed, and the materials sat untouched on the concrete slab for the entire length of his tenancy. I'm sure Bob didn't mean to leave the work undone. He didn't have bad intentions, and we didn't let it escalate to a conflict or anything. But even though we had agreed to the deal, we began to question whether we had made the right choice. What if Bob had actually completed the work? Would it have met our standards, or even code compliance? What if he stopped paying rent? Would we have felt bad to apply to evict him even though he had done all that work? Any way you slice it, this situation had too many possibilities for conflict.

It became clear to us that straying outside the boundaries of the tenant/landlord relationship was a risky mistake. Tenants should remain tenants, while contractors should stick to their role. Both relationships are distinct, with their own needs and expectations. If a tenant expresses interest in taking on work, it's crucial to carefully assess the situation. Is it worth the potential headaches and risks? More often than not, the answer will be no. We turn them down politely explaining that our company policies are strict on hiring tenants or allowing tenants to complete substantial work on the properties. We also blame it on insurance and liability reasons.

The same principle works in reverse. Occasionally, contractors we have strong relationships with will ask if we have any available units for rent. These requests always give me pause, knowing the potential strain it could place on our professional relationship. Fortunately, in most cases, they end up finding other housing solutions before I have to make a decision.

Dealing with conflict and navigating difficult decisions are challenges we all face, and they're something we try our best to handle with integrity and care.

We always try to pay our trades promptly—especially when they deliver great work and stick to timelines. But sometimes, things go sideways. A final invoice lands in your inbox, and it's way higher than the original quote. Now what?

This is one of those moments where your ability to stay calm and communicate clearly really matters. The first thing we do is go back to the original contract or scope of work. Were the deliverables clear? Were the prices firm or estimated? Sometimes it's just a misunderstanding. Other times, it's a case of scope creep that no one tracked properly. Either way, having it all in writing helps you approach the conversation with facts, not just feelings.

We also like to keep a paper trail—texts, emails, even voice memos if something important was said on-site. That way, if there's a disagreement, you're not left scrambling to prove what was or wasn't agreed on.

When we do have to push back on an invoice, we do it respectfully but directly. "Hey, this number came in higher than expected—can you walk me through what changed?" We've found that tone makes all the difference. Don't come in hot. Stay calm, even if you're frustrated. It's business, not personal.

If the trade has a valid reason, we're open to compromise. Maybe we split the difference. Maybe we ask for a better rate on the next job. And sometimes—if the relationship is rock solid, they have a valid reason and they've gone above and beyond—we just let it go. Or better yet, sometimes they're the ones who will let it go and readjust to keep us as a client. Relationships are worth more than nickel-and-diming over every line item.

But if the numbers don't make sense and they can't explain the jump, we ask for a detailed breakdown. That usually brings clarity fast—and keeps everyone honest.

In rare cases, when nothing else works and you really can't let it go, you might need to escalate. That could mean involving a third party, like a lawyer or mediator. But that's always a last resort, because the costs—financial and emotional—can add up fast. Once the issue's resolved, we always document it. In writing. No exceptions.

And then? We take the lesson forward. If the dispute came from a vague contract, we tighten up the next one. If it was from lack of oversight, we make sure to check in more often. Because every invoice issue is really just a systems issue waiting to be fixed.

TOP THREE TAKEAWAYS:

1. **Proactive Project Management Prevents Chaos:** Being hands-on and present during construction lets you catch small issues before they become costly problems. From foundation form errors to scheduling hiccups, your involvement helps keep things running on track. Good project managers don't just delegate—they observe, step in when needed, and keep trades moving in sync.

2. **Relationships Are Your Biggest Asset:** How you speak, respond, and treat your trades will shape your entire building experience. Show respect, communicate clearly, and don't be afraid to ask for their input. Build strong relationships— because when something goes wrong (and it will), it's the mutual respect that will get you through it.

3. **Problem-Solving and Communication are Critical:** From flushing policies to final invoices, clarity is everything. Set expectations early, put everything in writing, and don't avoid tough conversations. When disputes arise, stay calm, keep it professional, and protect your budget without burning bridges. Every issue is also a lesson that can tighten your systems and make the next project smoother.

CHAPTER 16

BUILDING FOR GROWTH: MOVING FROM HANDS-ON TO HANDS-OFF

As you already know, when we began our real estate journey, like many starting investors, we took on a big portion of the work ourselves in each project. In those early days, DIY was more necessity than choice. With little capital and no access to outside funding, taking on the work ourselves allowed us to save on labor and build substantial equity. Every building we designed, nail hammered, and wall painted taught us about construction from the inside out. The hands-on experience was invaluable, helping us understand the intricacies of every task.

But this approach came at a cost—one that extended beyond finances.

In Chapter 13, I broke down the pros and cons of DIYing. And I stand by those insights: DIYing can teach resilience, offer cost savings, and give you a hands-on understanding of your builds. But for us, the deeper story was about what that involvement started to cost us personally.

Our dedication, while instrumental to our success, took a heavy physical and mental toll. Rob especially faced repeated injuries, and both of us experienced a few burnouts—Rob more severely than myself. We began to see that while DIY had been essential in the beginning, it was starting to compromise the freedom we were working so hard to achieve.

THE TIPPING POINT: WHEN DIY STOPS SERVING YOU

We respected the process. We respected the work. We still do. And we don't regret starting out that way—it gave us our foundation.

But at some point, the stress, the exhaustion, and the constant juggling became too much. We were still trying to do it all: coordinate trades, source materials, swing hammers, and run the business. And then came COVID.

The pandemic delayed our plans to transition out of DIY. Costs went up. Trades became harder to book. Supply chains were a mess. And then, just as we were adjusting to that chaos, we found out we were expecting our first child. That was the real wake-up call.

We needed a healthier balance. We implemented set business hours—8 a.m. to 4 p.m., Monday through Friday—and hired a full-time general laborer, Isaac. That small step changed everything: our stress levels dropped, our marriage improved, and we finally had evenings again.

There comes a time when pulling back becomes the main necessity. The numbers might not look as appealing when you hire out. You might not build as much equity on paper. But what you *gain* in well-being, sustainability, and actual lifestyle freedom is worth far more in the long run.

After all, what's the point of building for freedom if the process steals it from you?

THE SHIFT FROM DIYING TO HIREING

As we began stepping back from full-on DIY, we created a new framework that would help guide us through the transition. We called it HIRE:

- **Harness resources**: Bring in experts who can do the job faster and better.

- **Invest in quality**: Skilled trades ensure high standards and reduce future maintenance costs.

- **Reassess regularly**: Keep checking in with your stress, schedule, and ROI—adjust when needed.

- **Empower others**: Build a team that supports the business so it doesn't rely solely on you.

We started by delegating smaller tasks to Isaac—jobs like flooring installation, which made more sense to hand off. Eventually he also took on the trim installation, cabinet assembly, maintenance calls and so much more. Today, he helps coordinate the site on top of everything else he does. With each step, we learned to let go—just a little more. It was hard at first, especially for two people who built every project like it was our own home. But it was liberating too.

We began to understand that true financial freedom isn't just about accumulating assets; it's about living a life that's healthy, balanced, and sustainable. That's when we truly moved from DIYing to HIREing.

THE ROAD AHEAD: BALANCING GROWTH AND WELL-BEING

In early 2025, we reached a significant milestone by hiring a Working Foreman, Justin, to manage day-to-day operations on-site. This was one of the best business decisions. The freedom this hire provided was phenomenal. It allowed us to shift our focus to the bigger picture—exploring new opportunities, securing financing, and planning future projects. It also gave us the flexibility to step away when needed, knowing the business could continue to thrive without our constant presence.

While we're still actively involved in decision-making and strategic planning, we've begun to step back from the full-time, hands-on work that once consumed so much of our time and energy.

Finding this balance wasn't easy, and it required a shift in mindset. At first, we assumed that hiring meant sacrificing profits. And yes, on paper, paying others may seem like it eats into your margins. But what we learned is that hiring strategically doesn't cost you—it multiplies your capacity. The sooner we brought in help, the sooner we could take on more projects, reduce construction timelines, and always focus on planning the next moves.

Instead of doing one build at a time, stretched over many months, we could run multiple projects in parallel. Instead of saving a few thousand on labor, we were now unlocking tens—or hundreds—of thousands in additional revenue by completing projects faster and moving on to the next one sooner.

When you hire the right people, it not only protects your time and well-being—it accelerates your growth. It turns your business from something that's limited by your personal bandwidth into a machine that can operate at a higher level. So while yes, it may feel like an expense, it's more accurate to see it as an investment—one with high ROI, especially if you're aiming to scale.

We have to trust the people we hire, give them the space and autonomy to do things their way, while still providing guidance, and building systems that keep everything running smoothly. And we've learned to accept that while sometimes things might not be done exactly how we would have done them, they're more often done just as well—if not better.

DIYing was the foundation of our journey, but knowing when to hire out has been just as crucial. It's important to reassess your business regularly, and transitioning to HIREing as soon as you can should be your goal.

We still respect the DIY approach—it's how we started, and we wouldn't be where we are today without it. It provided a strong start, but scaling requires stepping back. It's about striking the right balance between hands-on involvement and strategic delegation. By doing so, you can build a business that supports the life you want, not the other way around.

HIRING A VIRTUAL ASSISTANT (VA)

The shift from DIYing to HIREing wasn't limited to physical labor. As we moved away from day-to-day tasks, we also saw the importance of streamlining the *behind-the-scenes* work—things like managing schedules, emails, organizing all the paperwork, bookkeeping, payable accounts, and handling tenant management. This administrative side of our business had grown with each project and was taking up as much of my time as the on-site tasks were taking up Rob's time.

Recognizing this, we realized the need to extend our HIREing strategy into the digital space. That's where virtual assistants (VAs) came into play. Just as skilled trades allow us to focus on growth in the field, virtual assistants help us manage the administrative load, letting us focus on strategy, business development, and project planning.

We hired our assistant, Danick, at the beginning of 2024, and we couldn't believe we hadn't done it sooner. He started working 16 hours a week for us, and by Q3 of that year we had increased his hours to 25 hours a week, until he was full time by the start of 2025. We paid him 25$/hour and he bills us every two weeks. Sure, you could probably get an assistant that charges less, but in my experience when trying out cheap assistants through UpWork, they came at a high price of low skill and even less knowledge. At 25$/hour however, our VA is worth his pay. He is efficient, and has become just as emotionally involved in our business as we have. He takes pride in his work and cares about the outcome. We plan to negotiate his terms every year.

As someone who values efficiency and productivity, this section was co-written with him to explain how virtual assistants can revolutionize the way you work.

First, let's start with the basics: Imagine having a skilled professional by your side, helping you with administrative tasks, technical support, or creative projects, all without them physically being in your home (if you work from home like I do). VAs use tools like email, phone, and video calls to collaborate with you from their home office. From managing emails to creating social media content, virtual assistants can handle various tasks, making your work life easier and more efficient.

There are several types of virtual assistants and how they can support you:

1. **Administrative Virtual Assistants:** These multitasking wizards excel at organizing your schedule, managing emails, and keeping your business operations running smoothly.

2. **Technical Virtual Assistants** Need tech-savvy support for website maintenance, IT troubleshooting, or graphic design projects? You could have a go-to guy who specializes in small businesses looking to enhance their online presence and technical capabilities.

3. **Creative Virtual Assistants:** If you crave a sprinkle of creativity in your projects, there are creative VAs who can help with

content creation, social media management, and designing eye-catching marketing materials that set you apart from the competition.

4. **Multilingual Virtual Assistants:** For global reach and diverse linguistic needs, multilingual VAs can offer translation services, transcription, and customer support in multiple languages, bridging communication gaps and catering to an international clientele.

5. **Property Management Virtual Assistants:** Last but not least, I bet you didn't expect that you could hire a virtual assistant who manages your properties from a distance, could you? Well, we didn't either until now. With the right management software, emails, and systems in place, you can definitely hire a VA for just a couple of hours every week to help with tenant management! Music to your ears, right? Keep reading!

HOW VIRTUAL ASSISTANTS REVOLUTIONIZE THE REAL ESTATE INDUSTRY

The real estate industry has especially embraced the power of virtual assistants. Let's dive into how they transform key aspects like property management and construction administration:

Property Management

From screening tenants to marketing vacant properties, virtual assistants streamline essential tasks in property management:

1. **Screening Tenants:** VAs can help streamline the screening process for you by helping you conduct background and credit checks while also verifying rental history by calling landlords and employers for references. They can also double-check IDs, cross-reference previous addresses, etc.

2. **Handling Maintenance Requests:** VAs act as a point of contact for maintenance issues, ensuring timely resolutions and happy tenants. If you have property management software in place, it will make it easy for them to follow procedures, send the proper maintenance subs, and they can even call the tenants if

needed to troubleshoot the issues. (Bonus tip: If you're looking for management software, we use Buildium)

3. **Rent Collection**: Again, if you have management software, VAs can easily track rent payments, send reminders, and keep cash flow steady to minimize payment delays. If you don't have management software, you can have your VA create a checklist or a procedure for properly collecting rent by guiding them a little bit by how you've been doing them and asking them to find a way to improve the procedure. (Another bonus tip: You don't have to have everything figured out for them before they start working; you can absolutely give them the task of finding ways to make your business better by allowing them to create their own procedures for it. Often, by letting them take the initiative, they'll surprise you. They might already have the experience necessary to set your business up in a fraction of the time it would have taken you.)

4. **Marketing Vacant Properties:** By creating listings and engaging with potential tenants, VAs reduce the time you spend on your phone answering messages and repetitive questions from potential tenants. Instruct them on your qualification standards and the pre-screening questions to ask, then let them schedule showings that work for your schedule. Again, this is a huge time-saver.

5. **Creating and enhancing SOPs (Standard Operating Procedures):** See the following section of this chapter entitled "From Emotions to Systems, The Power of SOPs"

Construction Administration

In construction projects, VAs play a crucial role in budgeting, scheduling, procurement, and communication.

1. **Budgeting:** VAs help manage project finances, track expenses, and keep projects within budget limits. They can also handle accounts receivable and payable.

2. **Scheduling:** By setting deadlines and coordinating tasks, VAs boost project efficiency and minimize delays.

3. **Procurement:** VAs research suppliers, obtain quotes, and handle orders, call to have a port-a-potty and construction fence delivered on site, etc., ensuring a smooth flow of resources for projects.

4. **Communication:** Acting as a liaison, VAs keep all stakeholders informed, address concerns, and maintain effective project communication.

5. **Administrative Tasks:** There's always something administrative to deal with in construction/renovation projects. Whether it's managing utility companies (disconnects, reconnects), getting proper insurances, creating checklists and procedures like SOPs to help the flow of future projects.

6. **Bookkeeping:** I could probably write an entire blog post just for this because it's typically a dreaded subject for most entrepreneurs. To keep it simple,: we have set up our VA to help us with bookkeeping by having a simple folder structure on a cloud server where we take pictures of our receipts and save them in the proper folder. Our VA, while also managing the billables, knows where to file everything in the correct folders so that at the end of the quarter, he can tally everything nicely and send it off to our accountant.

Consider having your VA create his own email within your organization, like "va-name@abcproperties.com" with his own signature block. Or even better, have a general mailbox created like "info@abcproperties.com" , that way if you end up switching VAs, anyone can come in and take over the mailbox. As your VA gradually takes on the task of sending all the emails and correspondence, the tenants and/or contractors will end up getting to know him or her and will start calling them directly for any issue.

Once, on a Sunday night while we were having dinner with family, there was a tenant that got locked out of his unit, and the tenant automatically called our VA for help instead of us. Our VA followed the procedures we had set, and we didn't even hear about it. This is the ultimate goal; for the business to continue going on without us. Thanks to our procedures in place, it only took 5 minutes of our VA's time. Even if he would charge us a minimum hour for this, (which he didn't but I told him he could have), the 25$ would have been worth every penny for an evening with the family spent unbothered.

TRICKS FOR EMPLOYERS WORKING WITH VIRTUAL ASSISTANTS

If you're considering working with a virtual assistant, here are some tips to maximize your collaboration.

1. **Clear Communication:** Keep communication open and transparent to align on goals and expectations effectively. I like to use voice notes (through a phone messaging app of choice) so I can easily and clearly give verbal instructions without it taking too much of my time to type things out and formulate properly.

2. **Set Clear Goals:** Provide your VA with clear objectives for each task to drive successful outcomes.

3. **Provide Feedback:** Offer constructive feedback to support your VA's growth and enhance their performance.

4. **Trust and Empower:** Trust your VA to handle tasks independently and empower them to make decisions when needed. Like I mentioned before, allow them to take the initiative on certain projects or tasks and let them surprise you.

5. **Invest in Training:** Where and when needed, pay for certain courses for your VA to enhance their knowledge and skills for better results in the long run. It might be a great return on investment.

6. **Just do it:** Stop wondering whether you should hire a VA or how to prepare for hiring one, just hire one and let things figure themselves out. Instead, start wondering what you're going to be doing with all that extra free time. Are you going to hunt for more deals, or are you going to take up yoga?

Still, I'd recommend starting with a short contract for a specific task or project. For example, you can prepare a list of potential clients or find the numbers of other local landlords (or you can have them do research and gather a list), and ask them to cold call these clients to sell your services. Or even cold call these other landlords to see if they have any properties they'd like to sell to you. See how they handle it before deciding if the VA is right for you or if hiring one is even something you want to continue pursuing or not.

From my experience, embracing the power of virtual assistance can transform the way you work, boost productivity, and unlock new possibilities for your business. Remember, effective communication, trust, and role clarity are key to successful partnership, and this is more achievable when you set clear standard operating procedures (SOPs)

FROM EMOTIONS TO SYSTEMS: THE POWER OF SOPS

I was first introduced to Standard Operating Procedures (SOPs) during my time as an Administrative Assistant at Transport Canada in the transportation of dangerous goods division. Early in that role, about half of my time was dedicated to creating and expanding SOPs for our team's various duties. The goal was to build a clear, step-by-step manual so that anyone could step in and perform any role with minimal guidance, ensuring the organization could continue to function smoothly.

That experience taught me a valuable lesson: No one is indispensable, and a well-structured business must be able to operate without relying on specific individuals. When we started our real estate investing business, I knew we needed to apply the same principles.

Emotions often cloud judgment—whether it's the excitement of starting a new project, the frustration of unexpected setbacks, or the stress of tenant issues. Creating an SOP manual became our way of staying grounded. When faced with a tenant request that I would have previously felt bad denying, I could now point to our company procedures as the reason for my decision. It took the weight of emotional guilt off my shoulders and replaced it with logic and consistency.

To scale our business and protect our well-being, we knew we had to shift from emotionally driven decisions to a more systematic approach. Our SOPs now cover every aspect of the business—from screening tenants and handling rent collection to managing the administrative flow of our construction projects. Our assistant, Danick, helps keep these documents updated, ensuring they evolve with our business. And if you don't have SOPs already, this can be a great project to assign to your VA. Let them handle the tedious task of creating them.

SOPs are essentially step-by-step guides that outline best practices for various tasks. By establishing clear protocols, they remove guesswork and reduce day-to-day stress. For instance, bookkeeping. Instead of accumulating a mess with the construction invoices and expenses, we now follow a standardized process. It allows everything to remain structured and organized, and minimizes the risk of costly mistakes during tax reporting and budget reconciliation. Every team member follows the same procedure. Like McDonald's, where every burger is made the same way no matter the location, your business should run with that same level of consistency.

SOPs have been especially valuable in tenant management. When dealing with late rent payments, we no longer react emotionally or make exceptions on the spot. Instead, we follow a clear process: Step 1: reminders, Step 2: notices, and Step 3: legal applications. This objective approach minimizes stress and maintains professionalism.

Our SOPs are living documents that we regularly review and update. Assigning this task to a virtual assistant keeps the system current and provides steady work during slower periods.

Embracing SOPs has been a game-changer for our business. By standardizing our processes, we've improved efficiency, made better decisions, and created a more sustainable and scalable business model. This shift from emotions to systems has been crucial as we transitioned from DIYing to HIREing.

TOP THREE TAKEAWAYS:

1. **Transition from DIY to Hiring**: The chapter emphasizes the shift from doing everything yourself to strategically hiring professionals. While DIYing helped save money and taught valuable skills, it also took a toll on health and well-being. Transitioning to hiring allowed for better scalability, efficiency, and a healthier work-life balance.

2. **Importance of Delegation**: Delegating tasks to others, such as hiring a general laborer and later a virtual assistant, became crucial in managing time effectively and focusing on the bigger picture. The acronym HIRE (Harness Resources, Invest in Quality, Reassess Regularly, Empower Others) outlines the strategic approach to building a sustainable business by leveraging the skills of others.

3. **Implementing Standard Operating Procedures (SOPs)**: Transformed our business by shifting us from emotionally driven decisions to a structured, consistent approach. By standardizing processes like tenant screening, rent collection, and project management, we reduced stress, improved efficiency, and ensured our business could operate without relying on specific individuals. This system has been key to scaling our operations while maintaining quality and protecting our well-being.

CHAPTER 17

STRUCTURING YOUR ASSETS: WHY IT MATTERS

When you become a real estate investor, it's crucial to structure your assets strategically. This isn't just about taxes or paperwork—it's about protecting your investments, scaling your portfolio, and making your business easier to manage in the long run.

In the early stages, keeping things simple often makes sense. Purchasing properties in your personal name is straightforward and cost-effective. However, as your portfolio grows, structuring your assets becomes more important.

Proper structuring can:

- **Protect your personal assets:** Separating your business from your personal life reduces risk in case of lawsuits or financial issues.

- **Improve financing opportunities:** Some lenders may prefer lending to corporations, since most banks have stricter rules for individuals with multiple mortgages.

- **Create tax advantages:** While I can't speak to the technical side since I'm far from a CPA, there are strategies available that reduce your overall tax burden when structured properly.

As you build your real estate portfolio, two things are bound to grow: The opportunities for success and the risks you'll need to manage.

First, let's talk about risk. You want to make sure that your personal assets (your savings, home, etc.) aren't at risk if something goes wrong—

whether that's an issue with tenants, a construction hiccup, or anything else. By setting up separate entities, you can create a layer of protection. This means that if something goes sideways with the operational side of the business, your property assets are hopefully shielded. However, don't forget: No setup is bulletproof. If you don't maintain proper records or mix funds between the two corporations, you could lose that protection.

A well-planned structure can also offer some serious tax perks. For example, when we bought our Airbnb cottage in Quebec, since the property was already generating income it was considered a business. Therefore, it was the purchase price + sales tax. But since we purchased it as a corporation or partnership, we could defer that tax and only pay the purchase price. We will pay the sales tax only once we sell the property. Corporate structures tend to offer more flexibility when it comes to tax planning, and they may open up additional opportunities for deferring taxes on business income or capital gains. But remember, yes, you guessed it—talk to your CPA!

OUR JOURNEY WITH STRUCTURING

When we first started investing, we purchased properties in our personal names. It was simple, fast, and got us started. But as we grew, we realized this method had limitations. Banks started restricting our borrowing capacity. Most banks—and even most insurance providers—have a cap on the number of units you can finance or insure under the same personal profile. Typically that cap is anywhere between four to ten rental units, depending on the lender and jurisdiction. For us, that number was seven rental units. Once we reached that threshold, the banks either outright refused us or pushed us toward their commercial lending departments.

That's when we decided to incorporate. Our lawyer and our accountant recommended setting up both a holding corporation (to hold our properties) and an operational corporation (to handle construction and day-to-day expenses). This added some complexity, but it also gave us more flexibility with financing and added protection.

In addition to protecting assets, this setup allowed us to optimize taxes. The operating corporation, with its active income from construction projects, benefitted from the lower small business tax rate. Meanwhile, the holding corporation, which generated rental income, was taxed appropriately for passive income. This separation allowed us to structure our finances more efficiently, taking advantage of tax incentives specific to each type of income.

Moving from personal to corporate ownership essentially created a new financial profile when applying for funding at our bank. Although our personal credit history still played a role early on, the corporation was able to establish its own creditworthiness over time. This separation allowed us to access financing options tailored to business needs, often with higher loan limits and more flexible terms. Additionally, some commercial financing products are only available to corporations, further expanding our options as the business grew.

This structure made the most sense for us, given our local tax laws and business goals. The transition was not without its challenges—there were administrative costs, legal fees, and a steep learning curve—which still remains to this day. Still, the long-term benefits outweigh the hurdles.

However, structuring isn't one-size-fits-all. We've met investors with all kinds of corporate or partnership structures. Each has its pros and cons, which is why I strongly suggest speaking with a legal or accounting expert who can guide you based on your goals and your situation.

If you're not ready to incorporate yet, consider other strategies to keep growing your portfolio like using JV partnerships, leveraging HELOCs, or using private lenders.

JOINT VENTURE AGREEMENTS

If you're considering taking on partners or entering joint ventures (JVs), it's important to integrate this into your asset structure thoughtfully. A JV is typically formed for a specific project or series of projects where partners combine different strengths—such as capital, land, development experience, or management skills—to achieve a common goal. While a JV itself is not a separate legal entity, it can be structured within an entity like a partnership or corporation for added protection, clearer roles, or tax benefits.

For example:

- **Simple JV Agreement:** Just a written contract outlining terms—no separate entity.
- **Incorporated JV:** The partners form a new corporation together, giving the JV its own legal identity.

- **Partnership JV:** The JV is set up as a formal partnership with its own registration and tax considerations.

For our first joint venture, we had extensive discussions with both our legal and tax advisors. We agreed that it was most efficient for both parties to create a simple straightforward agreement that included our existing holding corporations. Opting for a JV instead of forming a new partnership or corporation simplified future exits and streamlined accounting processes. Our JV agreement also includes an appendix, which can be updated as needed with the addresses of properties we acquire and develop together.

KEY CONSIDERATIONS FOR JOINT VENTURES

1. **Roles and Responsibilities**: Clearly outline who is responsible for what. Whether it's securing financing, managing construction, or handling tenant relations, ambiguity can lead to conflict. Be as specific as possible in defining duties to avoid misunderstandings.

2. **Compensation for Services:** Assign clear dollar values to specific services provided by each partner. For example, if one partner is taking on project management, bookkeeping, or tenant screening, consider outlining a fair payment structure. This ensures contributions are valued appropriately and helps prevent tension over workload imbalances.

3. **Profit and Loss Sharing:** Agree on how profits and losses will be distributed. Will it be proportional to each party's contribution, or will there be a different arrangement? These terms should be spelled out explicitly in the agreement.

4. **Decision-Making Processes**: Establish how decisions will be made. Will there be a unanimous vote, or will one party have final say in specific areas? Defining this process is essential for avoiding stalemates in the future.

5. **Dispute Resolution**: Even with a well-structured agreement, disagreements can arise. Include provisions for dispute resolution, such as mediation or arbitration, to address conflicts before they escalate.

6. **Exit Strategies**: Planning for exits is a non-negotiable part of any JV agreement. Circumstances change, and partners may wish to sell their shares, dissolve the venture, or transition into new projects. Establishing clear terms for buyouts, property sales, or dissolution will save significant stress and financial loss down the road.

Either way, never forget to plan for exit strategies. Your asset structure or your partnership should facilitate not only your current goals but also your future plans. Whether you aim to sell your portfolio, pass it on to family members, or transition into a different investment strategy, a well-planned structure can make these processes smoother and more tax-efficient.

No matter your goals though, life has a way of reshaping them. Markets shift, partnerships evolve, and personal circumstances change. I'd recommend a yearly sit-down at a nice restaurant (tax write-off—wink, wink) to discuss your goals, revisit your agreement, and make any necessary adjustments. Build in flexibility where possible, and always have backup strategies in mind to adapt to unexpected changes.

QUESTIONS TO ASK THE EXPERTS

When you meet with your CPA and lawyer to discuss how to grow your business the right way, have them explain all the types of structures available to you. During the discussion, consider asking the following:

☐ **How can I protect my personal assets from business risks?** As your portfolio grows, how can you structure your investments to limit liability exposure? Exploring strategies like corporate structures, insurance policies, or placing properties in separate entities may provide added security.

☐ **What structure will make expansion easier to manage?** Consider whether a holding corporation could help streamline the process of building and managing multiple properties under a single entity, or if separate corporations for each project or for each action (building vs holding) would offer better asset protection and flexibility. Each option has different tax, liability, and administrative implications, so it's important they explain the difference of each.

☐ **How can the business remain flexible for future investments?**
As your portfolio grows, you may want to diversify or scale up. Whether you're building new triplexes, multi-family units, or transitioning into larger developments, your structure should be flexible enough to adapt to these changes without major overhauls. Flexibility is also crucial if you plan to explore joint ventures or future partnerships.

☐ **What are the tax implications of each option?**
Ask the experts how your asset structure will impact both your liability and tax strategy. With BTR, certain structures may help limit personal liability if issues arise with construction projects, while others may offer tax advantages on rental income. Understanding these implications is key.

☐ **What's the best way to manage cash flow between entities?**
Once you establish multiple corporations or separate entities, how can you efficiently move funds between them? For example, should you set up a formal management agreement where your operational corporation charges a management fee to your holding corporation? What's the most tax-efficient way to handle expenses like maintenance, renovations, or payroll across different entities? Understanding these strategies can help you maintain organized finances while maximizing cash flow.

☐ **Can you explain the best way to maintain the funds and transactions between corporations?**
Make sure your accountant guides you on how to properly handle transactions, including which accounts to use for different expenses and how to keep everything separate and in check. Then incorporate these in your SOPs. It's also essential to have a good bookkeeper who understands your type of structure and can help you stay organized. Maybe your CPA can refer someone that would be a good fit for you.

☐ **What are the ongoing compliance and administrative costs associated with managing multiple corporations?** Managing multiple entities involves annual filings, record-keeping, and corporate governance practices, which can be time-consuming and costly. Ask them what the average annual costs would be for those. How can you help ensure that the benefits of the asset structure outweigh these administrative costs? What are the best practices for staying compliant with changing regulations, and do you recommend specific software or support for managing these tasks?

Navigating corporate structures, tax strategies, and cash flow management is complex. Getting their expert advice and setting up your business properly from the start can save you time, money, and potential headaches down the road. However, I know the hourly rates of these experts can be steep. Which is why having these kinds of questions ready before the meeting can keep the conversation focused and save some time. Just make sure they can at least provide you with a ballpark figure of the costs before entering into any "transaction" with them.

A friend of ours once sought legal advice for a complex issue with the city regarding zoning regulations and development charges. After a few email exchanges, one in-person consultation, and a meeting with the city, he nearly fell off his desk chair when he received the lawyer's invoice for close to $9,000.

I've learned that asset structuring is less about finding the "perfect" setup and more about finding what works best for your situation at each stage of your investing journey. Don't let fear of complexity stop you from starting— but when the time comes to grow, take the step to speak with the experts.

TOP THREE TAKEAWAYS:

1. **Asset Protection & Liability**: Structuring your assets, such as incorporating, can help protect your personal assets from potential business risks, like lawsuits or financial issues. Separate entities for each project or corporation offer a layer of protection while improving flexibility in financing and management.

2. **Financing Flexibility**: A well-thought-out asset structure can improve your financing options. Incorporating can help overcome borrowing limits tied to personal profiles, allowing access to more flexible financing terms and higher loan limits, especially as your portfolio grows.

3. **Scalability & Flexibility**: As your portfolio grows, a well-structured business will facilitate easier expansion. Corporate structures provide flexibility for joint ventures, future investments, and tax planning, making it essential to have a structure that can adapt to changes and new opportunities.

CHAPTER 18

RISK MITIGATION CHECKLIST

The Build-to-Rent Strategy is complex, presenting both unique challenges and significant advantages. While the potential for a steady income and long-term growth is appealing, you have to conduct risk mitigation practices at all times to safeguard your investment. That goes for any business. This chapter is not so much a chapter, but more of a simple quick guide for risk mitigation practices. Even though I have covered them at various points, consider this your summarized checklist.

Hint: The last point is my favorite because it's controversial.

✓ **Do Your Due Diligence Early**

Before buying land, do thorough research. This means pre-consulting with your city's planning department and your financing broker, reviewing neighborhood demographics, and making sure there's solid rental demand. You want to be confident the property aligns with both your goals and the market's needs.

✓ **Know the Legal Landscape**

Make sure you're in full compliance with zoning bylaws, building codes, and rental regulations. Skipping this step can mean costly delays, fines, or worse—issues that could have been avoided with a bit of upfront effort

✓ Run the Numbers

A detailed financial breakdown is a must. Factor in your land cost, soft costs, closing costs, construction expenses, and potential income. Don't forget your exit options either. A solid financial model helps you stay grounded and make confident decisions.

✓ Structure to Protect Yourself

Use the right corporate and financing structure to protect your personal assets, reduce taxes, and open doors to better financing. It's not just about building—it's about building smart.

✓ Insurance at Every Stage

Set up insurance at key points: liability for vacant land, builder's risk once you break ground, and general contractor coverage if you're acting as your own GC. After the build, switch to a comprehensive landlord policy. Each policy should match the risks of the phase you're in.

✓ Have a Construction Buffer

Things will go sideways—delays, price jumps, surprise soil conditions. Plan for it. Keep 10% of your construction budget in a contingency reserve and reassess as you go. This is one of the biggest things that saves people from panic.

✓ Don't Skimp on Construction Quality

Cheap materials or rushed trades can cost you way more later in repairs, vacancy, or insurance claims. Work with skilled, reliable pros and choose materials built to last. This protects both your budget and your reputation.

✓ Plan for Rental Hiccups Too

Once the build is done, your property becomes a business. Set aside 3–6 months of operating reserves to cover repairs, vacancies, or economic dips. It gives you breathing room and helps you avoid emotional decision-making under pressure.

✓ **Screen Tenants Like a Pro**

Reliable tenants make all the difference. Run full background checks, verify income and past rentals, and trust your gut. You can manage this yourself or hire a good property manager (more on that in Chapter 19).

✓ **Have Rock-Solid Lease Agreements**

Clarity prevents conflict. Spell out payment terms, responsibilities, and expectations in your lease. A well-written lease saves a lot of back-and-forth down the road.

✓ **Stay on Top of Maintenance**

Deferred maintenance costs more later and drives good tenants away. Set a routine schedule, respond quickly to issues, and keep your property in top shape.

✓ **Avoid Putting All Your Eggs in One Basket**

It's easy to get stuck investing in one area, especially when things are going well. But diversifying geographically helps you hedge against local economic shifts or changes in regulations.

✓ **Know Your Exit Before You Start**

Are you holding long-term? Planning to sell after a refinance? Leaving room for future condo conversions? Think ahead so you're not boxed in when life or the market changes.

✓ **Keep Sharpening Your Skills**

The market is always shifting. Stay informed by reading, listening to podcasts, watching for policy changes, and learning from other investors. The more you know, the fewer mistakes you make.

✓ **Do not over-leverage:** This might be the best tip of them all. Overleveraging and continuously re-borrowing on existing properties to acquire new ones might seem like the smartest and fastest way to grow, but it can also be very risky. Want proof? Just look at the effects of the rate hikes in 2023. People who had more debt than income went from positive cashflow to completely negative, while some were unable to stay afloat, leading them to sell their properties.

I'll conclude this checklist with two quotes from a book called The Road Less Stupid by Keith Cunnigham.

> *"It turns out that the key to survival in the business world is how flexible you are in response to changes in the market or the environment."*

And finally,

> *"Survival requires more curiosity and less arrogance; more humility and less need to be right; better questions and fewer answers."*

CHAPTER 19

FOR THE DIY LANDLORD: CHEAT SHEETS!

When we first became landlords, we assumed the hardest part would be finding good tenants. Turns out, the real challenge was learning how to manage those tenants effectively.

I know this is not a book about property management, but for those of you who have taken on the role of a DIY landlord, I want to share some valuable insights. As you can imagine, being a DIY landlord is not all Skittles and rainbows. It's not just about cashing cheques on the first of every month. It involves managing people's homes (and indirectly, their families) by collecting one of their largest monthly payments. You will inevitably face challenges despite your best efforts to be fair, follow the law, and be the best possible landlord.

We've always managed our properties independently, but in 2022, we decided to try outsourcing to a property management (PM) company. At the time, we were juggling a challenging tenant situation while also adjusting to life as first-time parents. Bringing on a PM provided us with more freedom and peace of mind, though, like any new arrangement, it came with a few bumps along the way.

After a few situations where the management didn't meet our expectations, combined with rising interest rates in 2023, we decided to reevaluate our approach. With four of our properties being due for rate renewal, we gave the PM notice in the summer of 2023 and restructured our tenant management system. We implemented a professional application system and hired our VA to support the process. We returned to in-house management but with a stronger plan in place.

I'm not saying we won't ever go back to a third-party property manager, but we now see growth potential and cost savings in maintaining an in-house team with our own systems and procedures. After reviewing the numbers, the math simply made more sense for us.

For example, let's say a PM company charges 10% of gross income. If your portfolio generates $100,000 a year, that's $10,000 in fees. Depending on your workload, hiring a part-time VA at $25/hour may only cost you half that — plus they can assist with other tasks if needed.

As your portfolio grows, so does the impact of these costs. Suppose, after a few years, you've grown your portfolio to 30 units. If you're averaging $1,400 per unit each month, that's $500,000 in gross income annually — meaning you'd be paying $50,000 in PM fees. Alternatively, you could give your VA a raise to $25/hour for 20 hours a week, costing only $24,000 annually. With efficient procedures, your VA shouldn't need the full 20 hours for 30 rentals, giving them capacity to support other parts of your business as well.

Years later, as your portfolio grows further to a gross income of $1,000,000 annually, a third-party management company would cost $100,000. Instead, you could increase your VA's hours to full-time (40 hours/week at $25/hour), totaling $48,000 per year. Or even better, switch from a VA to a local hire who can handle even more tasks for you, including all the showings and turnovers. For us, the math simply didn't justify third-party management costs.

Today, we have about 40 units. Our VA works full time, but only because we still need assistance with construction processes and bookkeeping. Otherwise, for the number of units we have, a full-time assistant wouldn't be necessary. We also have a contract with my mother to handle turnovers. This arrangement allows our VA, who works remotely, to continue focusing on virtual tasks, while my mother handles only the in-person responsibility: showing units to prospective renters.

When tenants give notice, we pass the details to my mother. She steps in to handle communication, advertising, showings, and coordinating turnovers. Once the new tenants have their keys, her role is complete — until the next turnover arises.

Remember that despite having full-time people working for you, the key to success is to have well-documented processes and the right mindset. As soon as you become a landlord, you're running a business. So, remember to approach it accordingly, leaving emotions *out* of the equation.

REQUIRED DOCUMENTS

As a good landlord, you must maintain open communication with your tenants, keep a written record of every conversation, and have an organized filing system. Avoid relying solely on verbal agreements, and always follow up with written or signed documents. You can never be too vigilant.

Always ask yourself, if this were to end up in the landlord-tenant court, what would I need to make my case? The answer is always: documentation, written communications, dates of events, photos, *proof.* Remember that even the slightest issue can somehow escalate months or years later. Be thorough and be organized.

Here are a few steps to help you effectively manage your rental property:

1. **Rental Applications:** Provide both electronic and printable application options for your tenants. We use a Google Form for this, which works great because it includes all the required fields and attachments. This setup ensures applicants can't skip important sections or submit incomplete forms. As a result, you receive fully completed applications, making it easier to screen them against your criteria. I'll cover screening procedures in the next subchapter.

2. **Verify References:** Once you've received an application that passes all your criteria, verify the tenant's references from current and past landlords and employers. Have a reference form ready to record the answers you receive during reference checks. Store the reference forms and applications in an organized filing system for each tenant and a general file for all the applications you've received.

3. **Lease Agreement:** The lease agreement is the most important document in a tenancy. Make sure the lease is ironclad and specific to your local rental laws. Here in Ontario, the provincial government has a standard lease that every landlord must use, specific to the Tenancy Act of Ontario. If your area does not have standard forms, you can call your lawyer, or a local property management company or even a realtor, and ask if they can send you a template. You may need to pay a fee for this, but look at it as an investment. Without it, it could cost you thousands of dollars if you lose in court due to having a badly written lease.

4. **Additional Terms:** Even though we have a standard provincial template for our lease agreement, we are able to include additional terms to the template. Some of them are general terms that we include with each unit, like smoking and pet rules, and others are specific to the units in question.

5. **New Tenant Orientation Guide.** This document should outline your policies and the tenant's responsibilities, the importance of timely rent payments, and avoiding potential issues. You can send this along with the Lease when you are entering into the agreement. We usually send it to them with our Welcome Email package about three weeks before they move in.

6. **Move-In Checklist**: This is a short checklist of things they need to do to receive their keys to the unit like sending proof of insurance, sending confirmation that utilities have been switched over to their name on their designated move-in date, and sending the first month's rent before your key exchange appointment with the payment instructions. (This checklist is also sent as part of the Welcome Email package two to three weeks prior).

7. **Walk-through Report:** Before you give the tenant their keys, conduct a walkthrough of the property and fill out a walk-through form together. **This document is very important**. It can protect both parties in case of disputes and can serve as a point of reference at a later time. Take pictures if necessary and **have the tenant sign the form**. Send a copy of the form along with the photos to the

tenant, and store the original in their file. You can retrieve it and use the move-out column when they decide to leave.

This document has helped us settle disputes a couple times. It's similar to when you rent a car, and the company makes you walk around the vehicle to notice any pre-existing scratches or bumps, so you're not held liable. Or, that you are held liable if you do bring it back with a new scratch that wasn't there before. This document provides a general idea of the unit's state before and after the tenancy. Minimal wear and tear is expected, but actual damage is not.

8. **Document maintenance requests.** We now use a tenant management software called Buildium that easily tracks the maintenance requests, but before that we used the maintenance sheets. Basically, when a maintenance request is made, we would fill out a maintenance form and send it to the tenant via email. You could also send this form to the trade that is going to be hired to fix the problem. We would include pictures of the issue along with a description.

    Don't forget to keep all communication via email to maintain a clear written record. This protects both parties in the event of a dispute.

These documents are found in our website's Toolkit download.

HOW TO SCREEN POTENTIAL TENANTS

When selecting tenants, having a set of screening criteria is essential. Never rent your unit to the first person who expresses interest without conducting a proper screening. Even if finding the right person may take several weeks, always take the time for screening. We made the mistake of skipping this step in our early landlord days, and we learned the hard way.

Before showing the property to prospective tenants, I strongly recommend **pre-screening**. This means having a list of questions ready to copy and paste from your phone when responding to messages of interest from your rental ad. This helps to filter out the many messages you will receive and focuses on those who are serious and most likely to qualify.

My list of pre-screening questions included some of the following:

- ☐ Why are you moving?
- ☐ Are you familiar with the location of this unit?
- ☐ Who would be living with you?
- ☐ Does anyone smoke?
- ☐ Do you have pets?
- ☐ How many vehicles do you have?
- ☐ How long are you looking to rent for?
- ☐ This unit will be ready by *May 1st*Does this work with your timeline?
- ☐ (optional) Can you supply your appliances?
- ☐ (optional) You noticed this is a top unit and does not have access to a basement? or You noticed this is a basement unit?

Some people don't even respond to me, and on rare occasions, I even encountered individuals who were insulted by the questions. Although that reaction may seem like a bad thing, it just means the questions are working. They're weeding out those who are not a good fit. If you get insulted by me asking these simple questions, I don't even want to think about how hard it would be to deal with you as a tenant. On the other hand, those who are polite, answer all my questions, and agree to the terms, are given a time to view the property.

Don't forget that you're running a business, so don't be shy or embarrassed to ask these questions. It's part of your process and just proves to potential renters that you care about who lives in your properties.

To optimize your scheduling of property showings, I suggest booking appointments in 15-minute increments within a specific time frame. For example, on a Saturday between 9 a.m. and 11 a.m., If I have a few that are interested, I try to have someone booked every 15 minutes during that time slot. I try to do it this way to minimize the disruption on the current tenants (if it's not a vacant unit), and also to manage my time better so I don't have to go do showings every single day at odd times.

I will confirm the appointment with them the day before, and if they don't reply or they cancel, I won't hesitate to replace them with someone else. Despite my best efforts to confirm with everyone, there is always someone that doesn't show up. No big deal though since another person is scheduled just 15 minutes later. However, I do keep a record of those who fail to show without notice, as they often reach back out to me when I post a new rental unit later on. You can always give them a second chance, but in my experience, they won't show up that second time either.

Once the showings are complete and narrowed down to those few remaining who wish to proceed with an application, the actual screening begins.

This is my screening criteria:

☐ Everyone over 18 must fill out an application.

☐ Total household income is best if it corresponds to about three times the rent (this is not set in stone, but if I'm not comfortable with the total income, I may ask for a co-signer to add a layer of financial security and guarantee the rent will always be paid in full).

☐ They must be able to provide proof of that income: paystubs, bank statements, tax returns. Don't be shy, if anything feels unclear, request another form.

☐ References from landlords (previous and present) as well as from their current employer. We request a minimum of two references per person, and the outcome of the references must all be positive. I then cross-reference these names with my Realtor database to make sure the owners of the properties match the names. I do social media searches, check if they have friends in common that I might know and I also check if the references they included are not best friends or family members of the applicant by flipping through social media photos and comments. I know it's aggressive, but it's essential. Trust me.

☐ They must provide their credit report. Rather than pulling it myself and causing a potential hit to their credit score, I ask applicants to obtain their own report and send it to me directly. Most people can easily access their credit report through their online banking, and it won't affect their score. I don't have a minimum requirement for a credit score. I look at the overall report and application, and I use my best judgement.

☐ Credit history must be clear of any eviction or unpaid judgments from previous landlords.

In Ontario, there's a website called Openroom.ca where you can search the name of a landlord or tenant to see if they've ever been to the board before. You can also search the Landlord Credit Bureau website. Just keep in mind that these websites are not always up to date. Even though the applicant's name doesn't come up on these websites, it doesn't mean they have a clean history. We had a case at the Board with a tenant once, and the name doesn't appear on Openroom.ca for some reason, so these are not guarantees.

The criteria listed above may not give you a perfect tenancy, but since we started using this method, we have observed a significant improvement in the quality of our tenancies.

Credit checks are important to ensure there are no previous records of evictions. However, we do not consider credit scores to be the sole determining factor for a successful tenancy. In the past, we have had tenants with low-to-average credit scores who have consistently made their rent payments a priority and always paid on time. Exercise your best judgment during the selection process.

In our experience, one of the most critical aspects of a successful tenancy is the quality of the references. A simple conversation with the prospective tenant's current or previous landlord and employer can reveal a lot about their potential. This is often my deciding factor when the references are enthusiastic and genuine. On the other hand, if they sound rehearsed or monotone, as if they're not being negative but also not being positive, then there might be a red flag. Sometimes this is the person's way of saying, "Read between the lines and save yourself." I can often get these people a little more comfortable as I start to chat with them. You can try assuring them that the conversation is private and you will not be reporting anything they say back to the applicant. That usually helps to squeeze a bit more information from them. Don't forget to refer to the reference checklist from the link I provided above on what questions to ask a reference.

I hope this goes without saying, but it's important to emphasize that denying someone based on race, religion, sexual orientation, or any other form of discrimination is unacceptable. Treat all applicants equally and objectively, with the sole intention of finding a great tenant who will respect your property (and the landlord), pay their rent on time, and cause minimal to no disruptions.

A FEW MORE IMPORTANT GENERAL TIPS:

1. **Potential disturbances during construction**: When we first built units, such as fourplexes, we often rented the top units before the basement units were completed due to the way the zoning and permit process was done back then. When I would show the top units to potential renters, I would warn them about the potential for construction noise until the basement units were completed. When someone had moved into a neighboring unit, we were always careful about our hours of operation. We would work only during business hours, as per what we're allowed by our local bylaws. Just be mindful of this if you ever need to do the same for any reason. Respect your tenant's spaces.

2. **Post-construction warnings**: When a tenant moves into a unit we just finished building, I like to warn them about a few things when I give them the keys. First, dust may settle for a couple of months, and will be especially noticeable the first time they turn on the furnace or AC and the air gets moving. Second, the home has never been lived in, so its systems haven't been thoroughly tested yet. We may need to fix or adjust a few things, but that's normal. Finally, the building may shift slightly during the first year with the temperature changes and a few cracks will form in certain corners, walls, or even the

flooring planks. I tell them it's all normal and we will fix it when the time comes, or we may even wait until the end of the first year so we can fix all the minor cosmetic issues at once.

3. **Email communication ONLY**: I highly recommend maintaining all forms of communication with your tenant through email, unless there's an emergency. This should become standard practice once the lease is signed and should be included as a requirement in the lease agreement. Having a clear written record of all correspondence from the start of the tenancy to its end can benefit both parties. If we receive a phone call or text message, we will always follow up with a written email to document the conversation. Only once have I had tenants who were not tech-savvy, but with the help of a close family member of the tenant, we were able to continue with the email practice. Their daughter volunteered to receive emails on their behalf and even created an email account for them. Although the tenants never directly replied to the emails, their daughter always confirmed receipt and acted as a liaison. Overall, email has proven to be an effective and efficient method of communication, and has served as a great and easy way to reference back to previous conversations to confirm what was said, or not.

4. **Rental Laws**: Always stay updated with local rental laws. Be the master of this subject. Research and study them like you're preparing for a big test. Then save important or relevant local documents or references in an easy-to-find place.

5. **My Core Rule**: Treat every single one of your rental units as a business. Maintain mutual respect with your tenants, and as I've said before, leave your emotions at the door. Implement policies and procedures, and stick to them.

6. **Lockboxes**: We install a lockbox beside each unit door for maintenance calls, emergencies, or tenants who lock themselves out. The codes are kept private from our tenants and are changed if needed for security purposes.

7. **Other documents to consider**: We keep a maintenance checklist that includes when we last changed the furnace filters, cleaned the gutters, emptied the septic tank, etc. We used to have a rental master sheet (before the tenant management software) with all the units' PO numbers, tenant information, lockbox codes, etc. We also had a rent checklist that I would print and check off every month tracking who paid rent, in which account it was deposited, and what date it was received. We had rent receipt templates, a six-month inspection checklist, a move-out checklist, a move-out survey, and a co-signer agreement. Safe to say that having a management software saves you from having to do a lot of paperwork.

TOP THREE TAKEAWAYS:

1. **Managing Rentals as a Business**: Successfully managing rental properties requires treating each unit as a business. This involves maintaining detailed records, staying updated on local rental laws, and keeping emotions out of decision-making. Effective management includes having clear, well-documented processes, such as rental applications, lease agreements, tenant orientation guides, and maintenance checklists. A professional and organized approach helps ensure smooth operations and minimizes potential disputes.

2. **Importance of Screening and Communication**: Thorough tenant screening is crucial to maintaining positive landlord-tenant relationships. Asking pre-screening questions, verifying references, and conducting credit checks are essential steps in selecting reliable tenants. Additionally, keeping all communication through email ensures a clear and documented record of interactions, protecting both parties in case of disputes and fostering transparency.

3. **Adapting Management Strategies**: After years of self-managing properties, transitioning to a property manager provided insights into the pros and cons of outsourcing. The decision to return to in-house management, but with a team and professional systems in place, highlights the importance of adapting strategies to find a balance that offers freedom and peace of mind while maintaining control over the processes and standards.

CHAPTER 20

12 STEPS TO SUCCESS

I want to close this book with some mindset coaching to help you tackle your next goal with confidence and clarity. Whether you're a seasoned investor or brand-new to real estate, building mental resilience is critical. If you're experienced, you might be tempted to skip this section, but hear me out—mindset refreshers are always valuable, no matter where you are in your journey.

For those just starting, remember this: The moment you dive into real estate investing, you're stepping into the role of a business owner. Even if you've spent your life as an employee, it's time to embrace the challenges and freedoms of entrepreneurship. Every decision you make has the power to either grow or jeopardize your business. So, it's time to trade your employee hat for your entrepreneur hat.

The path to success isn't a straight road; it's full of potholes, detours, and challenges. Success belongs to those willing to put in the hard work—blood, sweat, and tears—before reaching the finish line. And for most entrepreneurs, that finish line keeps moving. We're constantly stretching our goals, pushing ourselves to achieve more. Even if your goal seems straightforward, it will likely take grit and determination to accomplish. As the saying goes, *if it were easy, everyone would be doing it.* So buckle up, buttercup! This journey is just getting started.

MY 12-STEP SUCCESS PROGRAM

I know the journey of real estate investing can feel overwhelming, but with the right mindset, it's possible to build lasting success. I made a 12-Step Success Program designed to provide you with a structured path to navigate the challenges, stay focused on your goals, and continuously grow both personally and professionally. Each step is grounded in principles that have helped me along my own journey, and I'm excited to share them with you. These steps will empower you to make better decisions, overcome setbacks, and ultimately create the life and business you envision.

1. **Define Your "Why" and Set Clear Goals, Then Define Your Business Mission.**

   Yes, I know I'm repeating myself, but this is essential: Start by defining your Why and setting clear goals. If you need a refresher, check out Chapter 2. Once that's in place, it's time to define your business mission.

   A mission is different from a goal. Goals can change as your business evolves, but your mission should remain constant. It provides guidance through your business's growth and evolution. Every decision should align with your mission to keep you on track and minimize mistakes.

   Our mission, for example, is to deliver quality rentals and provide excellent service to all residents, whether they plan on renting for a year or twenty. For us to maintain that level of service as we grow, our mission statement will remind us to focus not on the number of properties we have, but instead on the cash flow amount one property will generate. It reminds us that cash flow is key. We want to be able to afford to hire quality services if needed, without losing all our profit.

   So, let's say your Why is to provide a better life for your family, your goal is to generate $10,000 a month in cash flow, and your mission is to provide quality rentals. That's a strong foundation for a business plan.

A mission keeps you grounded as your goals and business grow. Clarify what you want to achieve long-term, beyond just numbers. Identify both short-term and long-term goals that support your mission. Make them specific, realistic, and flexible enough to adapt as your business evolves. Track your progress regularly and adjust as needed, keeping your mission statement in sight.

2. **Stay Educated**

Successful entrepreneurs thrive on knowledge, viewing education as a lifelong investment that strengthens their business acumen and keeps them ahead. While the goal is to become well-versed in every aspect of your business, it's essential to find the balance between expertise and the understanding that you'll never know everything. This mindset keeps you both sharp and open to continuous learning.

As a real estate investor, develop a thorough understanding of your market: Demographics, real estate trends, historical patterns, employment rates, tenant profiles, and local events that could impact demand. Legal requirements and rental regulations are equally essential, as they guide compliance and informed decision-making. By consistently building this foundational knowledge, you position yourself strategically for success.

Set aside time to read, attend industry events, and learn from seasoned investors. Experience will naturally deepen your skills, but prioritize ongoing self-education (and self-care, too). Pick up insightful books, research current articles, listen to relevant podcasts, and maintain a steady stream of useful information.

3. **Filter Your Mental Diet**

Think of your mind like a garden: Whatever you "plant" in it each day shapes how you feel, think, and act. Just as you'd choose healthy food for your body, it's worth being mindful of the content you take in—especially online. Seek out things that match your goals and values, like uplifting podcasts, books that inspire you, or articles that add value. This is what fuels a positive mindset and keeps you on track.

It's especially helpful to be mindful of what you take in right before bed. Your mind tends to focus on whatever you feed it last, letting those thoughts settle in overnight. A positive book or relaxing podcast can help you wake up with more clarity and motivation.

Over time, these small habits make a big difference. A *mental diet* filled with good information and positive vibes can make you feel more energized, and keep you aligned with the life you're building. Keep planting those good seeds, and watch how it boosts your happiness and productivity.

4. **Expect Setbacks**

Society teaches us that mistakes are bad, but in reality, mistakes can be good! They allow you to learn from them, fix them, and try again until you finally get it right. There's no better way to learn. It's normal to fear failure, especially when money is involved. You *will* make mistakes no matter how carefully you plan. But instead of worrying about failing to the point where you avoid taking any chances at all, try to anticipate it, learn from it, and quickly recover to try again.

Failures are a natural part of any entrepreneurial journey. When you see setbacks as learning opportunities, they become tools for growth. Expect the bad, but keep shooting for the best and view failures or mistakes as stepping stones toward success.

5. **Trust Your Instincts**

In the world of investing and building, challenges pop up all the time—big, small, and sometimes completely unexpected. There will be moments when even with all the data and research in hand, you'll find yourself in unfamiliar territory. That's where intuition comes in.

As an entrepreneur, you must learn to trust your instincts. Think of it as a tool in your decision-making toolkit. It's the voice that speaks up when data alone can't give you a clear answer or when timing matters too much to wait for every detail. When you've done your homework, analyzed the situation, and feel that gut sense telling you something—listen. Make a call based on the information you have and your best judgment, then commit to it and keep moving forward.

Trusting your instincts doesn't mean ignoring the facts or taking unnecessary risks. Don't just do something because Bob and Jo across the street did it. It's about combining your knowledge, experience, and intuition to make decisions *you* believe in. And remember, each decision teaches you something valuable, helping sharpen your instincts for the future.

6. Detach From Emotions

I can't stress this one enough, yet I still struggle with it. Emotions can be a dangerous thing in business. It's very important to know how to separate them from your business when you need to. Obviously it's easier said than done because we're not robots. Even though ChatGPT and I are best friends, (I call him Chad), there's no denying that we humans are far from AI and will always have some emotions to our actions. As long as you stick to data, rules, laws, numbers, implement thorough processes, checklists, criteria, and train yourself from early on to not let yourself get upset over the little things, you'll do fine.

Business demands clear thinking. Learn to separate emotions from decision-making, especially in high-stakes situations like tenant issues or financial decisions. Pause, step back, and make choices based on logic and long-term impact. If you get worked up about something, take a step back, take a breather and ask yourself: "Am I letting my emotions take over right now? If I take them out of the equation, what would be the outcome?" Nine times out of ten, a bad outcome can be avoided by asking yourself these questions and reevaluating your thought processes.

In his book *Never Split the Difference*, Chris Voss wrote, "As an emotion, anger is rarely productive — in you or the person you're negotiating with. It releases stress hormones and neurochemicals that disrupt your ability to evaluate and respond to situations properly. And it blinds you to the fact that you're angry in the first place, which gives you a false sense of confidence." Anger is just one example of a reoccurring emotion that should be diffused before being acted on, especially in a business context.

I know this takes practice, but try not to let the other party see you sweat. If you're unsure how to respond in the moment, hit pause. Tell them you need to consult with your business partner—or your legal counsel. And if you don't have either? No problem. Your "business partner" can be your dog. They don't need to know. What matters is that you step away, gather the right information, and come back with a clear, confident plan. When you do, lay it out calmly and objectively.

7. **The Importance of Team**

Success in real estate requires a team: Reliable trades, employees, advisors, realtors, a great lawyer, an even better CPA, and a solid support system (friends and family). Think of your team as partners in your journey who share your mission and vision. When you surround yourself with the right people, you gain not only expertise but also resilience and confidence.

Think of a relay race, where a team of runners passes a baton from one person to another to complete the race. Each runner has a specific role, whether starting the race, maintaining speed, or finishing strong. A team will help you tackle any project or challenge and propel you further, faster.

8. **Let Go and Delegate**

Like I mentioned before, getting your hands dirty and doing the front-line work yourself is good right from when you start. It will teach you many valuable lessons on how to steer the ship, but it's just as important to know when it's time to let someone else in and steer so you can get some rest. If you don't, the boat will eventually crash as you get overworked.

9. **Prioritize Health & Energy**

Real estate is demanding, but new construction can be even more demanding. You need both mental and physical energy to tackle this business. Start each day with exercise or meditation, fueling yourself to face the challenges ahead. Good exercise like a weight lifting routine promotes the release of endorphins, which can reduce stress, improve mood, and combat symptoms of anxiety and depression. It can also improve cardiovascular health by lowering blood pressure and reducing harmful cholesterol levels. This investment in health translates directly to lowering your stress levels, clearer thinking, better decisions, and sustained productivity.

Once you have the exercise habit down, you'll find that accomplishing your goals gets easier. You'll feel more energized and ready to take on life's challenges. Your brain will be more awake, and will be more able to find solutions and stay focused. You'll also sleep better and be generally happier.

10. **Network Authentically**

Forge relationships with other investors and entrepreneurs. Real estate success is about collaboration, not competition. Building a network of genuine connections means you have support, advice, and shared resources to draw on as you grow.

Networking is so important that, even when you don't feel like socializing, you should push through because it will spark up the energy within you. If you surround yourself with like-minded individuals — other real estate investors, business owners, and people more successful than you — you'll not only learn a tonne, but you'll be encouraged to go further. When you create a network of people who have been through similar issues, it can become such an amazing asset to have. Find your tribe and become limitless!

11. **Collaborate, Don't Compete**

Similar to Step 10, view other investors as allies, not rivals. Successful investors work together to exchange ideas, share insights, and support each other. Treat them as colleagues and help each other out. A positive reputation will carry you far. They might end up being excellent assets for your business. Usually, we end up becoming friends with every investor we meet in our community, while also developing respect for each others' businesses. We chat, we share stories, and we help each other out.

However, you should NEVER take advantage of other people's hard work. Word spreads fast in the investment and construction world, and people don't forget. It takes years of hard work to build a good reputation but seconds to destroy it, and rebuilding your network can be very difficult. Be honest, genuine, and upfront; don't expect anything for free and be prepared to give back. Only then will you become part of a great community and notice the real benefits that come from that.

12. Finally, Celebrate & Relax

It's a studied fact that overachievers, like most entrepreneurs, need vacation time at least twice a year to refuel that creative and "go-getter" part of the brain. No matter how busy you are or how small the victories may seem to be, always take the time to celebrate your wins and make a point of setting aside time for yourself and your loved ones.

The hustle is good, and I respect it, but if you don't find a way to enjoy the process at the same time, you'll end up resenting it and only slow yourself down. You'll also risk being unable to achieve your goals, and I don't know about you, but an inability to achieve my goals is not even an option for me. Not to mention your mental and physical health can be affected, and you won't gain anything from that. Give yourself breaks and stop when you need to stop.

OK, I think I'm done rambling now.

LAST WORDS

As you step into the world of Build to Rent investing, remember—this journey is about so much more than spreadsheets and construction timelines. It's about rising to the occasion, forging lasting connections, and one day looking back with a proud smile knowing you built something meaningful.

Every obstacle is a chance to grow. Every conversation is a chance to learn or build a relationship. And every win—no matter how small—is worth celebrating. When you lead with a growth mindset, you'll not only navigate the ups and downs more smoothly, you'll actually start enjoying the ride.

If you're just getting started, know this: with clarity, commitment, and a willingness to learn, there's no limit to what you can achieve. Set your sights on your first small win—whether it's researching a neighbourhood, connecting with a fellow investor, or walking a piece of land with fresh eyes. Stack those wins, keep showing up, and don't underestimate what you're building.

Even the smallest steps move you forward. So take them. Trust your gut. Stay curious. Stay driven. And most importantly—build not just for profit, but for the life you want to live.

You've got this. Now get out there and build it.

AUTHOR BIO

Natalie is a real estate investor, designer, and developer. She studied architectural technology and embarked on her investing journey in 2014 alongside her husband Rob by building rental properties from the ground up. Together, they have successfully constructed over 40 units, and counting, building themselves a multi million dollar investment portfolio before they turned 30 years old. They are continuously growing their business, working on bigger development projects as well as other investments. Natalie is passionate about all things real estate and loves to share her knowledge to inspire others to achieve financial independence through wise property investments and strategic development.

Your Feedback matters!

Thank you for taking the time to read this book.

I hope you found the insights and strategies
helpful. I really appreciate all of the feedback and
I love hearing what my readers have to say.

Your thoughts and experiences are
invaluable to me and other readers.

Please take two minutes now to leave a helpful review
on Amazon letting me know what you thought of the book.

Thank you for your support, and happy building!
- Natalie Cloutier

www.ingramcontent.com/pod-product-compliance
Lightning Source LLC
Chambersburg PA
CBHW061207220326
41597CB00015BA/1547